TRIUMPH
from FAILURE

ALSO BY ALISTAIR McALPINE

The New Machiavelli

Once a Jolly Bagman: Memoirs

TRIUMPH
from FAILURE

Lessons
from Life
for Business
Success

ALISTAIR McALPINE
AND KATE DIXEY

THOMSON

™

TEXERE

Australia · Canada · Mexico · Singapore · Spain · United Kingdom · United States

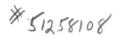

THOMSON

TEXERE

Triumph From Failure: Lessons from Life for Business Success
Alistair McAlpine and Kate Dixey

CONTENTS

FOREWORD

❧

"When a man has lost all happiness he is not alive.
Call him a breathing corpse."

—SOPHOCLES

E ACH YEAR IN INDUSTRY, billions of dollars are lost through the negativity displayed by both employers and employees. This negativity can start in the mailroom and end in the boardroom or, for that matter, the other way around. No matter where it starts, once lighted, it runs like wildfire through a factory, a company, even a country. More contagious than the flu, more deadly to a business than adverse financial conditions, negativity strikes at the very heart of our relationships with each other and makes us deeply unhappy. There is no difference whether you are male or female, employee or employer, married or single, negativity presents a real danger to the orderly passage of your life. Sadly, a mere resolution to think positively is no solution to negativity because the relationships we have with each other are far more complex.

In a search to make life happier, to defeat negativity, to allow our lives to run more smoothly, for our work to be more successful, and for those around us to feel a greater sense of harmony, we examine characteristics of everyday life that any person in any walk of life could attend to: kindness, rhythm, beauty, eating, sleep, failure, understanding, success, and imagination. We choose these features of day-to-day living with intent: to make happiness more readily available to anyone. This book is a short philosophical approach to happiness. There is no great universal truth that provides happiness, just a series of small actions that can be taken, each bringing us nearer to such a goal.

Since the beginning of civilization, ordinary people have struggled with unhappiness and philosophers have sought to explain and resolve this problem. The Roman rhetorician and speaker, Seneca, wrote, "Our aches and pains conform to opinion. A man is as miserable as he thinks that he is." In the opinion of Sophocles, the Greek playwright, "When a man has lost all happiness he is not alive. Call him a breathing corpse." Only recently have thinkers realized the extent to which personal unhappiness is contagious and how it can fundamentally affect a person's performance at work.

During the past twenty years, managers have been bombarded with different approaches to motivation in the workplace. The question is, what causes an increase in employee productivity and job satisfaction? What energizes employees to behave in productive ways? What channels and directs their behaviour? What forces in employees and in their environment reinforce or discourage them from following a particular course of action?

Let us suppose for just a few moments that the motivation for humans to work, lead, or follow is not to be found at the workplace but rather in the home and life outside of work. Let us assume that it is not an inspirational leader that makes a person perform efficiently, but a stable and well-balanced outlook on life in general. For many, the job has become a substitute for the aspects of their private lives that are distinctly out of balance.

This book is a chance to remind yourself about the simplicity of happiness and how to apply it to the various aspects of your life. Rhythm, beauty, eating, sleeping, failure, understanding, success, and imagination are all aspects of our lives that we can lay claim to and that are the foundation of our personal well being. Every day they determine how we approach our personal and working affairs and, most importantly, the decisions we reach.

*There are two sorts of achievements, those motivated
by hopes of success and those motivated by failure. The first
depends on a quest for excellence, which is healthy and mature.
The second is more pathological and immature. Winston Churchill
said success in life consists of going from one mistake to the next
without losing enthusiasm. Approach the great chain of life one
link at a time. The true art of success is learning how to cope
with failure, and understanding its enlightening rewards.*

—FROM THE INTRODUCTION

TRIUMPH
from FAILURE

"You can accomplish with kindness what
you cannot do with force."

—PUBLIUS SYRUS

Chapter One

CIVILIZATION'S CORNERSTONE: KINDNESS

KINDNESS IS THE FUEL of civilization, politeness and courtesy its etiquette, its formalities, and dignity its aim. Civilization is about responsibility for your own actions, and it is about tolerating other people's actions. One person trying to accept another's habits is the essence of civilization. Kindness typically reserved for the home and loved ones can be an attitude encompassing your entire life.

Kindness is a gentle, thoughtful, peaceful thing, most effective in its simplicity. Most humans have a tendency towards altruism—it has been proven in all parts of the world that part of the recovery process of disaster victims is altruistic behaviour. Lord Byron, the famous nineteenth-century English romantic poet, wrote beautifully of kindness, "The drying up a single tear has more of honest fame than shedding seas of gore." There is a gentleness to kindness that is noble. Kindness gives you not only strength, but also an inner beauty. The American philosopher and poet, Ralph Waldo Emerson, wrote, "There is no beautifier of complexion, or form, or behaviour, like the wish to scatter joy and not pain around us."

Kindness, however, is not just the stuff of poetry and poets; it is also the stuff of sound business sense. You never know to whom you are being kind. Kindness to an unfortunate may result in, and indeed often has turned out, to be repaid 100 times. The twentieth-century French writer, André Gide, had a view of kindness, "True kindness presupposes the faculty of imagining as one's own the suffering and joys of others." What Gide refers to here is, in fact, sensitivity. If you are to succeed in business, you need sensitivity, and sensitivity can be developed. In fact, "Kindness can become its own motive."

It should be easy to express kindness at work as opportunity abounds with typically large groups of people around you. People who show kindness demonstrate strength of character; it is admired and it is contagious. Importantly, kindness to your colleagues shows that you have confidence in your own ability, and shows that you have strength of character. Those around you will notice both of these and admire them. Both of these characteristics, strength of character and confidence, are qualifications for promotion. Admiration is totally different from popularity in the workplace. Bosses prefer to promote those who people admire and are often suspicious of those who are merely popular. Often it is believed that there is an emotional expense in giving kindness. People often avoid giving kindness in the belief that it makes them feel emotionally drained. These people are mistaken. The truth is, as we have to learn everything else in life, we must learn about giving kindness. Giving in a truly profound way is wonderful. If you really give profoundly, you will feel it in your heart and you will see it reflected in the people around you.

"We are made kind by being kind," wrote Eric Hoffer, the American social philosopher in the 1950s. And in the first century A.D., Publius Syrus, a Roman slave and mime, knew what some biologists and social scientists claim now to have proven, "You can accomplish by kindness what you cannot do by force." Kindness requires patience, an appreciation of the importance of others, a certain diplomacy. Compassion and kindness may sound sentimental but they actually lead to a deeper connection and rapport that create trust, a friendly atmosphere, compassion, and most importantly for business, an enjoyable synchronicity and harmony in the working environment. The people who are able to create such an environment and display these qualities are people who others trust to become a leader in the business world and the community

Leadership evolves out of expertise, ambition and luck, but true inspiration comes with a willingness to connect your own vulnerability with somebody else's. So do not pass up the opportunity to remain silent and caring if the need arises. This so-called "soft" management approach is the ability to make yourself open and sensitive to others' feelings. It takes courage to be quiet and listen to someone else's discomfort. This can feel strange within a working framework, but actually it forms a greater professional respect. The art of kindness is not just approaching a market challenge, but meeting the needs of each individual to find a resolution.

Kindness to those around you is important, but perhaps more important is kindness to yourself, the most difficult form of kindness to practice. Reward not only your success but also your effort. Kindness to yourself helps deal with rejection. You may get disheartened, and self-kindness alleviates frustration brought on by an initial lack of success. Often, other people do not want you to succeed, so self-kindness is not only important, it is necessary. You cannot get it from others. Kindness to those who fail wins appreciation. Kindness to those who win when you fail brings respect. Kindness is a building block of a happy life. Kindness is born in consideration and love. Teach yourself to be considerate, mostly in small matters, and consideration for others in big matters will become second nature.

In relationships of all natures, it is well worth remembering that your perspective of other people will change with the differing situations in which you find yourself. The memory of a life is made up of many small incidents. Even large incidents are made up of small incidents, some details well remembered, some half remembered; some, in the nature of folklore, are distorted fact and embellished fantasy—details invented that for you have become facts. These incidents, as the dots that comprise a photograph, are the picture of your life and become a complete memory. When the circumstances of your life change, the pre-eminencies of these small dots rearrange themselves and the picture of your life alters. Your attitude and perception change to issues and people. In extreme cases, heroes become villains and vice versa. In truth, however, they have not changed; merely how you see them has changed.

Kindness must always be meaningful. When you are pivoting in your life, it is easy to be confused about meaningful kindness. Just being lovely to everyone is no solution. Rather, as always, kindness must be carefully considered, directed with as full knowledge of the facts as possible. Haphazard kindness, as exemplified by the comedy routine of the boy scout who took an unwilling old lady far out of her way across a busy road to earn "a good deed for the day," can only cause confusion and distress. As Thomas Fuller, an African slave and mathematician, wrote in 1732, "Unreasonable kindness gets no thanks."

Kindness has its own rewards, for those who have succeeded in developing their instincts and sensitivity can physically experience the sensation of their own kindness around the area of their heart. The sensation is so memorable that it is astonishing. Yet we fear and resist that sensation, perhaps because we simply think that it will feel so good and then disappear, leaving us sad and disappointed, unhappy that this memorable feeling could come and go so easily.

As a sensation, kindness may frighten people. They are scared because they do not trust kindness in themselves or others. These people believe that there must be a catch in being kind. For them kindness is associated with weakness and brutal honesty, which they regard as an admirable quality but is actually unkindness. Often these people see themselves as "saying what they think." More often, they do not take the simple precaution of thinking before their victims hear what they have to say. These types of people believe that you are being kind to them only because you want something from them. They are sad people trapped in a sad suspicious world incapable of coming to terms with even the first building block in the construction of happiness.

Conversely, kindness quite often comes from a totally unexpected source, a person who you do not know well, and certainly did not expect to be kind to you. Even a total stranger can make an act of kindness to you spontaneously, just because they felt like giving more than was required. How wonderful you feel when a total stranger is kind to you; conversely, how wonderful you feel when you are kind to a total stranger. It is an amazing moment, sparked perhaps by an action that can be so small as to pass for good manners. The scale of the kindness does not matter. Kindness has a disproportionate effect on the well being of both the giver and the recipient. Samuel Johnson, the eighteenth-century English writer and thinker, is quoted in *Boswell's Life of Samuel Johnson* in 1781 as speaking well of spontaneous kindness. "Always set a high value on spontaneous kindness. He whose inclination prompts him to cultivate your friendship of his own accord will love you more than one whom you have been at pains to attach to you."

Learn to enjoy receiving kindness, learn to enjoy being thanked. It will make the giver of the thanks glow and it may produce a second or two of shyness, so intimate that it will touch the other person deep down inside. Enjoy the acts of giving and receiving, for they are moments of true beauty. The least expected these moments are, the greater their beauty. How strange it is that we so often receive kindness from the most unexpected sources and unkindness from those who we would most expect to be kind. Kindness over time, however, accumulates into a pile in our psyche and helps us come to terms with times when people are rude or unkind.

Kindness is fundamentally different from a desire to please, which is a deferential activity. Kindness is an instinct, mutual to two people. An instinct evolved in one returned by another in equal measure. Kindness is without doubt at least a layer of building blocks in the construction of happiness. Kindness and how you deal with others are closely intertwined. Do not make that smart remark that is devastating to the ego of others, forget it, put it out of your mind. Even to think of hurtful remarks colors your attitude to others and leaves a stain on your own spirit. Put aside the jibe that leaves even the smallest scar on your relationship with others. Avoid that verbal passage of arms, as the argument that often leads to sensuality is not to be confused with the path to happiness.

Needless to say, it is a lot easier to be kind to someone who is kind to you than to a person who is unkind to you. Kindness is not an abstract quality. To promise kindness and not to fulfil that promise is one of the surest ways to damage a relationship. Trust is suspended by such an action; you are left with a question mark over you in the mind of other people. Misused kindness, such as giving to take, is again an action that will break down trust, which is a basis for a satisfactory relationship. As Juvenal, a Roman satirist, wrote around the year 100, "Nature, in giving tears to man, confessed that he had a tender heart; this is our noblest quality." There are no dangers in kindness. People say to each other that you can be too kind, but this is untrue. There is no downside to kindness; you cannot lose through practicing kindness.

By being kind you show strength and attract people. People will want to work with you. They will think of you as being fair and confident. Other people will know that because you are kind you are not likely to make judgements based on petty biases and the prejudices of other people. Other people who you work with will know that you are your own person and in their confidence you will find encouragement and feel better about yourself. Even if your kindness is rebuffed and not reciprocated, however shabby the treatment you receive in return, your own kindness will fortify your spirit, enhance your life, and lead you towards happiness. You can never be too kind. Kindness is not a sign of weakness. As Franklin D. Roosevelt said in a radio address on October 13, 1940, "Human kindness has never weakened the stamina or softened the fibre of a free people. A nation does not have to be cruel to be tough."

*"I am fooling around and not doing anything,
which probably means that this is a creative period."*

—FREEMAN DYSON

Chapter Two

✍

FINDING YOUR RHYTHM

Timing in life is undeniably important and part of it is rhythm. Rhythm runs through all aspects of life, love, beauty, work, play, and politics. With the right rhythm comes careful decision-making, well thought-out plans, proper management, civilized behaviour, and happiness. Civilization, as we know it, depends on rhythm. The relationships that make up a civilized society depend on rhythm within that society.

In its most pure form, civilization is about behaviour, whereas opera or paintings are the trappings of civilization, not its constituent parts. Being late, for example, is an uncivilized kind of behaviour; it is an interference with the freedom of other people, a disruption of the rhythm of their lives. Constant lateness is very often a demonstration of someone's belief in their own superiority over the person they are to meet; the fact that it is just downright rude is too simple a reason to dismiss an action that has far deeper meaning and consequences for civilized behaviour. A person who is late and gets away with it will take other liberties with the notion of civilization. Timing is a part of rhythm, gratuitous lateness is an insult to rhythm. It breaks the rhythm of a relationship and creates tension where there should be harmony. A relationship with someone who has these habits, unless it is an extremely casual relationship, will not work at any level, whether it is personal, business, or social.

The rhythm of speech and music impact the rhythm of life. Music varies for the occasion and creates differing emotions and differing reactions. Music taps into our neural machinery. An orator uses rhythm to awaken anger, remorse, or delight in an audience. A comedian uses rhythm to make jokes work. Conjurers use rhythm in their magic; you watch one hand but the trick happens with the other hand. In many ways, life's rhythm is a conjuring trick; life is never quite how it seems. Composers use rhythm in their music. Ludwig Van Beethoven, the great composer, was stone deaf for most of his life yet he was able to write beautiful, emotional music that he could not hear. He could, however, feel rhythm, and what he wrote echoed the rhythm of his emotions. It is not by chance that the European Union chose Beethoven's Ninth Symphony, "Ode to Joy," as its anthem. The music speaks to us all with its rhythm and pitches that trigger corresponding high and low emotional reactions. Music impacts our moods in all areas. Even research on shopping malls tells us that when German music is played, more German wine is sold and the same for French music and wines.

A runner will jog faster with a definite and harmonious

beat as his legs move in time with the rhythm, whereas a mobile phone conversation would slow his pace. Anything that disturbs a rhythm will change the mood of a situation. Hit, bounce; hit, bounce; hit the ball and let it bounce. In sport, business, and politics, one side always tries to destabilize the rhythm of the other to outdo them and win an advantage. During the Wimbledon Tennis Championship, the English weather is unpredictable and matches are frequently halted due to rain. Many times the player who is two sets up returns to the court only to be thrashed by his or her opponent who has had extra time to reassess his or her game and break the other's pattern. In a casino when a gambler is on a winning streak in roulette, it is not because of the odds, which are a mathematical certainty. But rather, in practice, a momentum builds and a clever gambler spots this rhythm and uses it to change the odds to his advantage. Casinos are on the alert for this type of occurrence and quickly change the croupier because the human rhythm that builds in spinning the wheel can actually change the odds. Similarly, a certain rhythm will build when shuffling and dealing a hand of cards in bridge. The human inclination to develop a pattern is always present and variable, unlike a machine where a factory worker is forced to synchronize his movements as part of the manufacturing process.

Needless waiting is a disruption of rhythm. When waiting in lines, if the line moves at a steady or rhythmic pace it becomes a thing of no consequence and there is little tension. If a line stops and starts, tension builds and rhythm is destroyed. When waiting at traffic lights, some traffic lights change faster than others. Some drivers choose routes where there are faster lights. In a way, these people organize their lives to avoid stress. Traffic jams cause tension and destroy rhythm. Some drivers are always destroying rhythm by being in the wrong lane hesitating with their turn signals.

In other aspects of life, instant communication either destroys rhythm or speeds up rhythm, which makes it harder to cope with this new high-speed rhythm. Our environment is over-stimulating and it encourages us to have too many thought processes. Instant availability means that instant questions need instant answers, removing the time to think. Answers to questions asked in this way tend to be reactions rather than considered answers. As life becomes rushed, mistakes are made, misunderstandings occur that take time to rectify. And worse still, when computers and mobile phones break down, we are bereft. New technology and the new rhythm of our lives are both disrupted; we are therefore distraught and thrown into panic. Our lives become filled with tension instead of the happiness that comes from simply being out of touch.

The time of day is significant to rhythm. When you break bad news is as important as when you time good news. Hitler was aware of the dramatic impact of having conferences at dusk, as it is an extraordinary time of day. He called most of his meetings at dusk because he wanted the public to meet in the open air and experience the day changing to night. Dusk is the best time to indoctrinate people because they feel closer to nature. Neither light nor day, dusk is a time of general uncertainty that Hitler used to implant his own certainty in the minds of others, helped of course with dramatic lighting and the hypnotic music of Wagner.

In each day there is a time that is appropriate for certain things to happen, a time to sleep, a time to negotiate, and a time to travel. Effective management flows more smoothly when there is a fixed time for meetings each week. A designated time to troubleshoot the next eventualities, and looking beyond tomorrow prevents hiccups that stem the flow. This also allows people to prepare themselves, which waters the plant of professionalism. It is the uncertainties of life, the people who say "perhaps," "we will see," the "maybe's" that eventually slow your pace and upset your spirit, by their cowardice and lack of decisiveness. A feeling of relief is gained by coming to decisions. Regardless of the outcome of events, there is a great release of tension when a decision is made, yet making decisions often frightens people.

So many people prefer to hover through life as serial non-committers. These non-committers are exhausting; they live on other people's energy. Avoid them, they are a great waste of time. Always remember the time scale of our lives is short and in those lives we only have limited time frames during which we can achieve our necessary objectives. There is no time for unnecessary uncertainty or obstinate prevarication. *New York Times* journalist Thomas Friedman wrote in an early 2002 editorial, "We live in an age of continuous partial attention. Being fulfilled is about committing yourself to someone else or some experience that requires a level of sustained attention. And that is what we are losing the skills for, because we are constantly scanning the world for opportunities and we are constantly in fear of missing something better." This behaviour is widespread and spiritually depleting.

In our new age, our inner rhythm, the integration of the mind, the body, and the spirit is important because our ability to learn how to be emotionally fluid is of more relevance when there are far more facts moving around at a far greater speed. You need to be able to digest information, assess instructions, and maintain equilibrium as well as rhythm. Executives need to adapt to differing circumstances, to take time to relax and think. The twentieth-century American physicist Freeman Dyson extols the virtues of idle time: "I am fooling around and not doing anything, which probably means that this is a creative period." Switching-off time is beneficial on two counts, to create a vacuum that cleans the head and to let your body readjust, which precipitates new ideas. The notion of total originality is a denial of rhythm. Rhythm exists because one invention springs from another, one event is influenced by a past event, and one person has learnt something worth remembering from another.

The tempo of our daily life is a delicate thing even though it is created by seemingly mundane tasks. A rhythm is created by our domestic routines: getting dressed, driving, and eating. If you cannot find a rhythm at home, how on earth will you find a rhythm at work? First get your home life in order and your life at work will follow. Do not excuse your disrupted home life by believing that you devote everything to your work. Productive employees have bosses who have satisfactory home lives.

You do no one a favor by burying yourself at the office—your home life and then your work life will suffer.

Rhythm in any crisis is vital. Struggle to preserve your nocturnal rhythm and do not change your habits. The time scale of your problem will be far longer than you expect. That problem will take on an impersonal quality. The problem is not a massive criticism of you, but rather part of the cut and thrust of commerce. An experience such as bankruptcy is horrible but not terminal. Keep your natural rhythm and you will keep your money, self-respect, and your health. Ancient health philosophies from India and China are well worth studying for a better understanding of rhythm. For example, Indian Ayurvedic medicine divides mankind into three different types, Khapha, Pitta, and Vata, whose different temperaments require different eating patterns; whereas the Chinese maintain that the five elements of the universe, Earth, Metal, Water, Wood, and Fire, in each of us must be in balance for good health. In China, they believe there are particular times of day when an organ is more active—so it is sensible to eat between the hours of 7 and 9 in the morning, during the *active stomach* period. Hence the expression, eat like a king for breakfast. Knowing which elements are out of balance would help us to better understand each other; we could make allowances and better tolerate each other's moods. Fortunately, the greater public awareness and appreciation for Eastern medicines and practices is helping corporate executives manage stress levels. Using acupuncture treatments to stay in balance, for example, can be very effective.

Human mental concentration and synchronicity are more measurable today than ever before due to an extraordinary machine called a random event generator. Robert Jahn, a Princeton scientist, has conducted experiments with astounding results. On many occasions people throughout the world have prayed or meditated in unison, and now this can be measured by a machine. It appears that a global consciousness can be collectively monitored with this invention. One of these machines in New Jersey had forecast a major disaster nearly three hours before the first airplane struck the World Trade Center. The mechanism inside records two numbers, one and zero, in a totally unpredictable sequence rather like an electric coin flipper, which is printed out across the paper as a graph that usually shows a wavy horizontal line with minor alterations. This represents normal life, night and day, light and dark, constant normal fluctuation. Yet on the morning of September 11, 2001, the graph peaked like the Eiffel Tower. Strangely, it had started its steep climb from 6 that morning—three hours before the first hijacked plane hit the first World Trade Center tower. The uncomfortable sensation thousands of people experienced as premonitions of a disaster as they awoke, prove that they collectively altered the rhythm of the graph. There are forty of these machines all over the world that link up to a laboratory computer in Princeton. Resident scientists believe it was a surge in fear felt globally before the event, recorded by the generators, on the graph paper. During the funeral of Princess Diana, a picture of a mountain was drawn. A less noticeable but still distinctive one appeared during Mother Theresa's funeral. What a curious collective mind pen.

Rhythm is about breathing, and learning to breathe properly has a profound effect on your health. Breathing in sequence with someone you are trying to impress draws his or her sympathy to your words, you flatter them by adopting their rhythm, breathing so that your speech comes out in a matching tone. Breathing controls excitement and instills a level of rhythm to your life. Understanding the empirical reason for how people behave, or, in fact, taking in just the way they are, is a fantastic way of getting closer to a more realistic partnership. You gain respect by allowing people to be who they are and who they are not and particularly not expecting them to be who you are.

There is no doubt that the movement of the earth, moon, sun, and stars affect our rhythm, as does the changing of the seasons. Slowly in modern society, the natural definitions that these provide become less and less clear. The invention of electricity shortened night, the effects of sun are imitated, and the seasons have merged together. We have conspired to destroy the rhythm in our lives and have replaced it with the boredom of universal availability. Once it was necessary to travel to buy exotic goods; now the goods available on Madison Avenue are found in Singapore and the exotic goods of the East are found on Madison Avenue. A universality of shopping and food is coming close to a worldwide pollution adding to the ever-mounting tension in our lives. What rhythm there is left is speeding up to the point where it is in danger of self-destruction.

"Beauty is skin-deep."

—ANONYMOUS

Chapter Three

❧

ALLURING BEAUTY

ARISTOTLE, THE GREEK philosopher and mathematician, wrote in the fourth century B.C. that personal beauty requires that you are tall. Little people have charm and elegance, but beauty, no. These words would not have found much favor in Japan. While beauty is universal, it is also in the eye of the beholder, completely subjective, wholly a matter of opinion. A sense of beauty is colored by our mood as indeed it colors our mood. In 1764, Voltaire, the French playwright and novelist, wrote, "ask a toad what is beauty and he will answer that it is a female with the great round eyes coming out of her little head, a large flat mouth, a yellow belly, and a brown back."

Volumes have been written on body tattoos and ritual scarring—the scale of both these activities would lead one to believe that attempts to improve the natural body are universal. Shown for the first time ever in Paris's Louvre Museum are designs and styles that involve what the Western World once regarded as distorted limbs. Now they are commonplace and regularly ripped off on the catwalks of the world —Vivienne Westwood's bottom pads and Jean Paul Gaultier's transposition of sex are only two of a myriad of examples. Changing the face, degrading it with the heroin look, lots of black around the eyes, the tired, sick look popular with some models is just one of these styles. The world of contemporary pop has echoes of Ancient Egypt and its women of quality who painted around their eyes with kohl.

Hottentot women of Guana seem to many of us hugely overweight with bottoms so enormous that you could stand a tray of drinks on them. In their own country, however, this feature is considered a sign of beauty and wealth as their diet needs to be excessive to achieve the full impact of this shape. Food for these people is hard to get and expensive. It follows, therefore, that women who eat a lot and have big bottoms have access to great wealth. Yet, in New York today, it is necessary to be skinny in order to be considered fashionable and wealthy. Over size 4 and you are in danger of being a social outcast, whereas an x-ray woman in Guana would not be looked at by a potential husband.

The toned, tanned bodies of models who peer down at us from poster boards in our streets encourage self-criticism. We forget the photograph has been airbrushed to provide marble skin, smothered in moisturizer for the shine of limbs and painstakingly lit by an expert to throw a false sun and careful shadow. Fashion is a form of seduction that seduces those who practice it to a far greater extent than it seduces others. The Barbie doll manufacturer, Mattel, spent tens of millions of dollars researching the perfect face.

True beauty is not that of the Barbie doll, however; truer is the beauty of old age. The elegance of experience has a great beauty about it, calmness and certainty. The casual ability that comes with knowing how to do something well brings out beauty and real confidence. The last painting of Titian, the last operas of Verdi reverberate with their accumulated experience and universal acclaim that gave them the confidence to perform better than ever. Great dignity comes with coming to terms with ageing and the change a person must adopt as their image changes. Beauty increases as the spirit moves outwards towards the skin.

The honest beauty of youth and age, showing each for what it is, not hidden, not unnecessarily changed. Honest beauty that shows how the emotions are displayed on a face, a smile, a tearful look—these are things of joy and can only make you happier if you practice allowing them to come naturally. Don't hide your emotions like a Botoxed stare. It can be the unexpected aspect of a body, a peculiar shape that is alluring. It is the honest look that attracts, not a false face put on in the morning, rubbed off at night, not a face or figure bought from a catalogue. What you see is what you get, an openness in word, deed, thought, and fact—not the ugliness of meanness disguised as beauty. The beauty of generosity is far more beneficial to you and to others than a false beauty.

Our values of beauty are getting more symmetrical. Cosmetic surgeons remove a tired fatigued face by upturning the muscles and tightening the skin to make it look taut and young—the response is often that the person looks healthy when in fact the character lines have been removed. Often the character gathered over the years is removed in less than an hour in a different kind of theater. However well executed, the old saying "you earn your face" is true. Do not imagine that just by changing your face, you can change your heart and mind. The muscles of the face differ from any other in the body. They are known as memetic and attach directly from the bone into the skin, so the expressions on the face come from deep within the person. The muscles express the feelings of the person through many small movements in an extraordinary and profound way—they show sadness, anger, joy, or fear.

Distorting and changing the body has always been with us. A scar, far from destroying beauty, may be a point of attraction, as were the scars worn by students in Germany during the first half of the last century. Scars gained in duels with swords advertised both honor and courage as well as class. A scar from birth can give a face a quirky look. The ritual scars of tribal people denote manhood and bravery. The Flat Head Tribe of American Indians bound boards to their children's heads to give them a flat, receding forehead, an attribute that would be regarded as a sign of a manic mass murderer in the West but can also, as in Degas' bronze of the little ballerina, be totally beautiful. On top of that graceful figure with its bronze limbs, torso and red tutu skirts, Degas placed the head of a serial killer. The head, ugly in isolation, used in conjunction with the beauty of the bronze figure and the image of a ballet dancer, produces a startlingly beautiful sculpture. The long necked women of India who elongate their necks from childhood with bands of metal have an extraordinary beauty.

Physical shape is only a hint to how we are and can lead to an observer being badly misled. Mental shape is how we really are, and it is by balancing various mental aspects of our lives that we find happiness. Western cultures believe that a sturdy body is an honest body, the emphasis being on manual labor or honest toil. Well-defined masculine muscles are a sign of physical, sexual power and, in a sense, this may be right, for a muscular dancer will probably be a more athletic and active lover than someone whose body is not athletic. This does not, however, mean that they will be a more imaginative lover than the person with no athletic ability. Long fingers are considered to belong to philosophical hands; brains, however, are in the head, not the fingers. Short, strong fingers belong to people who make things. The calluses on hands, for instance: A callus on the inside of the second finger of a right-handed writer's right hand is an indication of a trade, but should that writer type then the sign would not exist. All this, however, is about justification, a perception of a person based on an idea for an increased level of gratification. To seek gratification by searching for types likely to provide that gratification will only gain frustration. The physical shape and how we change our physical shape is an indication of a mental change that is taking place inside us.

The work ethic in how fashion and beauty manifests itself is very important. It is the same work ethic that plays such an important part in our lives, often filling us with great clouds of guilt. Caucasians of the wealthy and educated classes had their robes made with extra long sleeves to demonstrate to all and sundry that they did no work. Clerical workers, who for the nineteenth and most of the twentieth centuries, regarded themselves superior to manual workers, wore clean white collars, which, had they done any manual work, would have lost both their stiffness and whiteness. Manual workers wore blue overalls, a color that hides both dirt and the cheap material it comes in. This divided the two sets of humans with a border that was hard, and for most of that period, impossible to cross. Today, in the West, the boundaries between humans are gone but prejudice in both directions still exists. Only people who are able to remove all prejudice from their minds will be able to relax enough to enjoy beauty, an important aspect in the construction of happiness.

Frustration comes from feeling prejudice just as it comes from practicing prejudice. How we look, in our age, is the surest way to invite prejudice. How other people look is the surest way for us to feel prejudice. This is not an emotion that comes from jealousy, although jealousy may well play a part in it. This prejudice comes more from the much-used phrase "I don't care for the look of him or her." Rough hands that once seemed to denote a lower class or working-class person actually can be extremely beautiful. For example, look at sculptures by Rodin: hands in bronze, knuckled and rough but of a beauty complete in themselves, detached from a body, owing nothing to any other shape or texture. Perfectly manicured hands, once considered educated and upper class, have no real beauty to them when detached from an elegant body. This applies to all broad generalizations. When your body changes, others' perception of you will change, for how we look is the shorthand used by others in the recognition of who we are. Contentment is accepting people as they are and not insisting that they are as you would have them.

In search of beauty, and through beauty a path to happiness, it is necessary to consider man's relationship with nature. Man, in his own creations, competes with nature. To find happiness, people need to come to terms with both the power and vastness of nature. It is, however, only through paying homage to nature that a built environment can have any chance of offering satisfaction and happiness to those who inhabit these man-made places. By appreciating and understanding nature, knowing its role in our lives, we can affect both how we feel and how we think. Nature is in the vastness of deserts, terrifying in its stillness; it is in the cozy peace of a country garden, the sudden violence of an earthquake, flood, or forest fire. The respect paid to a mountain by those who live in the shadow of a volcano is enormous, especially in regard to their acceptance of the inevitable. Order, rhythm, purpose, balance, and proportion. The best in architecture and gardening has all of these and the results are wonderful. The greatest gardens of the world have an order, a rhythm, and a purpose. They are, in fact, models of life.

Nature influenced classical architecture. Each of the classical orders came from nature in one form or another. Thus classical architecture has a pleasing beauty as a result of its continuity of nature. This architecture introduced balance and proportion with the lines of those who designed, built, and used it. It became a mainstay of stability and most important in their well being and general happiness. For example, Corinthian columns were created by the accident of a tile put on a grave and on top of the tile a basket containing an offering. By chance, underneath the tile was a seedling of the Acanthus plant, which grew and its leaves began to curl. So the Corinthian order of architecture was born, reproduced by Greeks, Romans, and generations thereafter to top the columns that supported their buildings. Doric columns originated from the way that pieces of timber were joined together. Rustic timber and bits of trees were used without removing them from their natural habitat but by shaving and shaping their surfaces. The Romans were so aware of the connection between architecture and nature, they even used columns from ruined cities to roll the land after they had planted the seeds—the seeds of next season's harvest. In time, the symbolism of this action was not lost. In the eighteenth century, these same rollers were placed around the philosophical gardens as markers of this memory from the past and later still in the twentieth century used by architects and designers, such as Lutchens and Gertrude Jekel. This same urge and instinct, after all, was the one that motivated those who built the great philosophical gardens of Europe and the Far East in an attempt to capture the world, its myths and realities, in a microcosm.

Whether a person realizes it or not, the positive action of creating a garden will bring that person closer to the reality of their lives. Their actions are not just a way of prettying a patch of ground or filling up a moment in the tedious emptiness of a weekend. As with the person who comes to terms with the terrors of vastness in a desert, garden making, on whatever scale, is an action fundamental to the well being of their lives, for the power of nature must always be remembered for being far more powerful than we can possibly imagine. Even though, in terms of posterity, gardening could be considered futile, or a temporary delight, as no garden is as old as the Egyptian pyramids, the act of gardening is the first attempt to emulate nature in proportion to our lives.

Beauty is subjective, and true beauty is not a physical attribute, but rather a sense that you develop within yourself, a sense that you communicate to others. One of the necessities for developing this inner sense is a desire to understand both the beauty and nature of others. There can be no doubt that if you desire to find happiness, it is better to surround yourself with happy people. In the same way, the environments where you live, work, and play must also be conducive to happiness. Johann Wolfgang von Goethe, the nineteenth-century poet, novelist, and philosopher, got it right when he wrote on April 18, 1827, that "beauty is primeval phenomenon which itself never makes its appearance but the reflection of which is visible in a thousand different utterances of the creative mind, and is as various as nature herself."

*"When a man's stomach is full it makes no difference
if he is rich or poor."*

—EURIPIDES

Chapter Four

THE GLAMOUR
OF FOOD

HUNGER IS SELDOM the reason for eating these days, at least not in the Western world. Rather, the presentation, the color, the shape, and sculpture of food are vitally important to us. Foods that we believe to be beautiful tempt us. Foods that we regard as ugly repel us. Snake is an example. We in the West have bad feelings about snakes both dead and alive. We have no desire to touch them, let alone to eat them. In Vietnam, snake is such a popular dish that Hanoi alone has nearly a thousand restaurants that sell only snake. So popular is snake as a delicacy in Vietnam, that the place is becoming infested with rats due to the absence of snakes to control the rodents.

Epicurus, born in 314 B.C. on the island of Soros, was a Greek hedonist, materialist, and empiricist, who thought long and hard about happiness. He also published over three hundred books on happiness and various other subjects involving the living of a satisfactory life. To quote Epicurus' words, "the beginning and root of every good is the pleasure of the stomach; even wisdom and culture must be referred to this." Epicurus, however, drank water rather than wine and was happy with a meal of vegetables, a piece of cheese, and a handful of olives. "Send me a pot of these so that I may feast whenever I like," he wrote to a friend. Simple as his tastes may have been, Epicurus was careful with whom he dined. "Before you eat or drink anything, consider carefully whom you eat or drink with rather than what you are to eat or drink, for feeding without a friend is the life of a lion or wolf." There is no joy in eating alone, and positive harm is eating with people who are negative.

Today, when families are spread across the globe, meals are casual—with the fridge a more popular meeting place than the dining room table. Where there was once order, there is now confusion; where there was once discipline, there is now freedom. So we must, in our minds, replace the formality of childhood with a discipline necessary to cope with contemporary freedom. Meals in the past became part of a structure that brought stability to a person's existence. Through this day-to-day formality, each person knew his or her role in the family. They may not have liked their roles, but they knew and understood their positions. Food taken at regular times, in specific amounts and varieties, provides the structure that we need. The happier your body is, the happier you will be: neither too fat nor too thin, not a couch potato or fitness fanatic. Discipline is applied to food in order to provide good health and then a chance to enjoy happiness. In any Western restaurant today, you'll find the exact opposite of a routine procedure for eating.

At least a hundred people will be practicing the Western habit of talking with their mouths full or swallowing in double quick time in order to get the next word out.

The smell of food is often the very last consideration to tempt us. Flying food in the form of canapés at a party tempts us further—we have to catch it as it moves around the room, we eat with our eyes. Anytime we are eating when we are not hungry, we are eating to fill an emotional need. Munch when your body requires fuel rather than in the supermarket before you have actually bought the product.

While people in the Western world are generally becoming more aware of the effect the food they eat has on their health, junk food still flourishes in contrast to the carefully prepared confections of great chefs. Chefs now fancy themselves as artists quite as much as they consider themselves as cooks. Food and our attitude to that food in the Western world have become concerned with glamour, the visual aspect overtaking taste as the criteria of quality. Surprisingly it is now possible to feel special sitting and eating your meal in a restaurant that seats 1,499 other people. This is quite a trick, proving that the pleasure you feel is in the mind rather than on the palate. Restaurants flourish today as never before. They are bigger and flashier, the décor as important as the food (they are the theaters of today). These restaurants, often giant in size, trade on reputation, built by a combination of a glamorous book of their recipes and reports in the press of the important people who go there. Tables are booked months in advance. One restaurant in London, The Ivy, has a two-year waiting list for a table. The proprietor, when asked whether a table booked for two years hence could be left in the client's will to a relative should he die, was nonplussed.

When eating in capital cities avoid empty restaurants, when eating in rural Italy greet an empty restaurant with joy for the chef cooks only for you. A visit to a restaurant has become a habit rather than a treat. The demand greatly exceeds the supply of fashionable places to eat, while those once fashionable restaurants languish empty and finally close. People are impressed by fashion rather than food. If you are taking someone to a restaurant, it had better be a fashionable one. The social cachet of being able to get a table at short notice in the restaurant of the moment is immense. A meal planned weeks ahead however, let alone two years, takes the edge off the event. After waiting that long, the meal must surely be an anti-climax. The habit of dining in a smart restaurant has become an anthropological, spectator sport. As celebrities are spotted at close proximity, their every look and action is dissected. Because we believe these celebrities to be special, we feel that we are special by being so close to them. The excitement of arriving at a restaurant where photographers are waiting outside doesn't go unnoticed by those who have waited three weeks to get a reservation. It's the other customers who are quite as important as the food. To sit at the next table to Madonna and eat a hamburger is more highly regarded than to sit alone eating the finest confection of a capital city's greatest chef.

While all this is intriguing and will likely set the adrenaline pumping, it does little for your general well being vicariously living through other people's habit patterns. Sitting a few feet away from a great celebrity in a friendly restaurant or club may well add spice to our existence; it is not, however, an existence in itself. To let yourself believe that such things as these can be an existence or even an important part of that existence is an act of self-delusion on a grand scale.

Meals are about eating, not merely meeting, talking and drinking. Brooks Atkinson, the twentieth-century journalist and theater critic for *The New York Times*, in 1951 wrote, "The cocktail party has the form of friendship without the warmth and devotion. It is a device either for getting rid of social obligations hurriedly en masse, or for making overtures towards more serious social relationships, as is the etiquette of whoring." Izaak Walton, a great (perhaps the greatest) fisherman, was more sanguine about parties. In 1865 he wrote: "I love such mirth as does not make friends ashamed to look upon one another next morning."

It is one of the great paradoxes of modern life in the Western world that all the while more people eat in restaurants, more people are spending fortunes on the latest gadget for the kitchen. More often than not, people with elaborate kitchens will, when they dine at home, serve ready prepared or takeaway food. Cooking at home is in danger of becoming a lost art. Cooking can be therapeutic and relaxing. If you approach this task in a logical way and proper manner, it concentrates the mind, removing all other thoughts. Cooking can make you feel better about yourself, as well as other people feel better about you.

Even when many people do cook at home, they eschew fresh produce in favor of frozen or convenience foods. It is important to be aware of what we are eating and the story behind the ingredients so that we have a real appreciation of the extent to which what we eat impacts our physical well being. Chicken is the most widely consumed domestic fowl today and take only nine weeks to grow large enough to feed five people. Before the Second World War, it took twenty weeks to reach that size and the meat was far less tender. Cheap chickens grow even faster reaching the right size in six to eight weeks. Their cruel discomfort should shame us into not purchasing them. Artificial lights are switched on and off startling them—is it night or day, so their growth hormones kick in even faster. In fact they are often standing on broken legs from the weight of their ever-expanding bodies that grow so fast. There is a never-ending conveyor belt full of grain for them to peck. After being slaughtered, plucked, and chilled, they are packed and delivered, ready for the retailer and then the consumer. This journey is known as the cold chain.

"Globesity" is the nickname for the epidemic of obesity spreading at an alarming rate, from the industrialized countries of the West to the developing ones, where it is side by side with malnutrition. The World Health Organization found that obesity has increased by fifty percent worldwide in the last few years. Sub-Sahara Africa is where most of the truly hungry live and where famine and infectious diseases dominate the general health of the poorer countries, but now in the developed countries, obesity brings with it a rise in diabetes, cancer, and heart disease, plus serious digestive disorders. You only need to stand at a North American airport to see the true scale of the people who travel. These people who travel have wealth, and clearly from the shape of them, many consume large quantities of the wrong sorts of food.

"Sleep and confidence are almost the same thing,
they both come together."

—UGO BETTI

Chapter Five

✍

A GUIDE TO SLEEP

U GO BETTI, the twentieth-century Italian dramatist, touched on the true nature of sleep in 1949 when he wrote the afore-mentioned words. He echoed similar sentiments of Heraclitus, the pre-Socratic philosopher, who in 500 B.C. wrote, "Even sleepers are workers and collaborators in what goes on in the universe." We should never be ashamed of sleep. Sleep is a fabulous and miraculous journey we undertake every night after the sun sets and as the sun rises.

When Thomas Edison invented the light bulb in 1879 he was well aware of the implications of his invention, boasting that he only required four hours of sleep per night. Oil lamps produced the phrase "burning the midnight oil," and as this was expensive, soon after it became dark, work would stop. So Edison separated light from fire, and electricity meant we were moving away from the rhythm of nature. Now we work shifts—night-shifts and weekends. Some shops are now open on Christmas day as well as late into the night. The result is that our sleep time has dropped about twenty percent in the last century and we have at least one and a half hours less sleep per night than our great-grandparents. This has led to one of the much-neglected problems of contemporary life—sleep deprivation.

It was thought, centuries ago, that man's vision of the soul came from sleep and the dreams of ancient peoples. Many people believe your spirit leaves your body whilst in slumber and wanders about, returning later. And if you wake up with a start or feel you are falling through the air this is the spirit re-entering the body. Dreams are partly the brain's way of tidying up what has been occurring in a person's life. We don't always remember our dreams—but recurring dreams can become an issue and it needs to be realized that these dreams might contain a message for you to learn and understand. If you have a problem just before you go to sleep you can ask for help and there may well be a solution in the morning. Under no circumstances should you engage in mathematics after sunset or you will find it extremely hard falling into a refreshing sleep. It is not the length of time that you sleep but rather the quality of your sleep. In the words of Publicus Syrus, written in the first century B.C., "He sleeps well who knows not that he sleeps ill."

Longevity is associated with quality sleep, which helps boost your immune cells, and this leads to greater vitality in your waking life. If you are to be happy then a proper pattern of sleep is necessary. If you are to be efficient in carrying out your daily employment then a proper sleep pattern can only help this to happen. Without a sleep pattern that suits you, there will be a loss of efficiency, a poor work product and a strong sense of unease and failure. The sense of failing to perform as you or your employees would wish brings unhappiness, and a cold, hard, nagging misery, which in time becomes your norm. A constant tiredness couples with a sense of dissatisfaction.

Our society's trends reinforce our sleepless culture. Drowsiness while driving leads to endless fatalities. Many businesses stay open late to accommodate other business's timetables. People work late only to leave their desks and party later. People check their emails late at night and check them again early in the morning thereby missing yet more precious sleep. Sleep is necessary for recuperation even while travelling. Using artificial stimulants, such as vast quantities of caffeine or cocaine, of which there are traces to be found on a large number of money in circulation, does not take the place of sleep. From the shop floor to the boardroom, there is a great deal of evidence that cocaine is taken to boost energy and confidence, the tell-tale signs of which are fast-talking, excessive sniffing, and mood swings. These types think no one will notice, yet they are the ones who need sleeping pills to counteract the other chemicals.

Tiredness is often the cause of mistakes. With tiredness comes the need to bring matters to a conclusion, however disadvantageous that conclusion may be. People are more often than not motivated by tiredness. Tiredness is a condition that affects every aspect of your life, a condition easily recognized yet extremely hard to accept. It is only too easy to pretend to yourself and others that you are not tired. You, above all people, have an inexhaustible supply of energy. You are not frail as others are, you can keep going when others fall by the wayside. Ignoring tiredness is folly, a form of self-delusion inherent with danger. In fact, it's easy to keep going when you are tired, but the product of your efforts however will fall in direct relationship to your tiredness. Stop and rest, even if it's only for a few minutes. Sleep, start again and the standard of your work will be all the better. A person's work should be measured by quality, not the length of hours spent working. During the early 1970's, the British Government, in a moment of self-inflicted crisis, imposed a three-day working week. Contrary to expectations, production on building sites rose to the point where the outputs for three days were matching those for five. Life was better for the workers, profits better for the employer. No sooner was this crisis over, however, and the work ban lifted, than the unions and employers agreed to return to five days of work.

Habit is a hard taskmaster, and the puritan work habit of the Western world is deeply embedded in most of us. Tiredness is not just a physical condition. You can wrongly equate tiredness with boredom. The dull feeling that you get from boredom is often mistaken for tiredness; after all, you often yawn and feel sleepy when you are bored. People often mistake tiredness for dissatisfaction. Equally, dissatisfaction soon leads to tiredness. There is no happiness in tiredness. There is, however, great happiness in a job well done, a sense of satisfaction and relaxation which has nothing to do with tiredness, but is often mistaken as a pleasant form of tiredness.

Six great hours of sleep are far better than eight hours where you toss and turn as your mind slips in and out of gear. If you want a good night's sleep and have no doubt that without it you will not produce your best work, then stop thinking about problems, for solutions that come in the night are seen in the morning light as the greatest of miscalculations. When you wake in the night and your thoughts are whirling around, write them down, get them out of your head onto paper; this kills them and sleep comes. Worrying, however, at night about something you can do nothing about, is pointless. Always remember, a thought that is horrendous in the darkness and loneliness of the night is often a small thing in the hubbub of the day. Go to bed with the attitude that you have done the best that you can that day. Think about an achievement, however small, then turn your mind off, clear your mind of your own affairs. This takes practice, so do it when there is no crisis in your life, when your work and home lives are running smoothly. Set a pattern to your sleep when all is well and it will be easier to maintain that pattern when you have problems and the going gets tough.

The physical conditions of how you sleep are as important as the mental attitude to sleep. The right mattress, pillows, linen, the right sized bed, a comforter that suits you, all are important. Your comforter may well be different from the comforter of others. The joy of sliding into your comfortable bed is symbolic of a day well spent. The colors and the patterns that you sleep in will have an effect on you and how you sleep. Red is sexy but too active a color to help you relax. Blue is a cerebral color, useful for thinking. Black is dramatic but impractical for dust, and other stains will show up on black bed linen. Green is calming, yellow is for courage and white is the most neutral and refreshing. Pillows need to be arranged on a bed to make it look inviting. While a television is a convenience in a bedroom, it is also a distraction, for a television is adept at turning night into day. It is a mistake to watch horror movies late at night, particularly in the bedroom. The double bed can be full of negative thoughts. You can feel desperately alone in bed with someone just a touch away. You must care about the person you are in bed with. Not to care about them is taking risks with your whole relationship, especially if your companion is part of a regular relationship.

Sleep is the most important way of spending your time. Ovid, the Roman poet, got it wrong in his first book of collected love poems, *Amores,* where he wrote, "What is sleep, but death warmed up." Sleep is a joy that needs working on to reach its ultimate possibility. Thomas Wolfe, the twentieth-century American author of *Look Homeward, Angel,* wrote in 1935, "In sleep we lie all naked and alone, in sleep we are united at the heart of night and darkness and we are strange and beautiful asleep, for we are dying in the darkness and we know no death."

Sleep at its best is a state of contentment. Luxuriate in the pleasure of sleep. Never feel guilty that sleep is time wasted. So often, when we are awake, someone says something or we do something that makes part of our insides contract; actual happiness is an expansion of our insides. If, for instance, we all took deeper breaths—most of us breathe in short breaths, or spent more time in stillness, then we would find a deeper sense of both physical and mental peace. People who meditate or do yoga actually do have a state of contentment that is real. As we have thousands of thoughts a day, and maybe as many as 20,000 on some days, a life of simple meditation is just not practical in a working life. The rest of us, however, come as close as we are likely to get to this state when we learn to sleep properly. Lord Byron was another poet who understood the beauty of sleep and its ultimate joy. He wrote in 1816: "Sleep has its own world, and a wide realm of wild reality, and dreams in their development have breath, and tears and tortures and the touch of joy."

"We may stop ourselves from going up but never from coming down."

—NAPOLEON BONAPARTE

Chapter Six

~

THE TRIUMPH
FROM FAILURE

NAPOLEON WAS WRONG, of course, as we will demonstrate later in this chapter. For now, suffice it to say that
Napoleon lost power but he left an indelible mark on France,
Europe, and the world. The philosophy of despair can be
found in the Yiddish proverb, "He that lies on the ground cannot fall." This splendid idea that if you do nothing, take no
risks you will be all right is fundamentally flawed, for if no one
sticks their head up then the parapet will need to drop lower
and lower. Max Beerbohm, the twentieth-century caricaturist,
realized that there is something special about failure: "It is more
interesting than success."

In 1927, Elbert Hubbard, American editor and writer, wrote,
"The line between failure and success is so fine that we scarcely
know when we pass it, so fine that we often step on the line and
do not know it." The man put his pen on it, for we do not really
know the difference between failure and success. We believe that

we are quite clearly one or the other when in fact we are elements of both. And how do we find out if we are a failure or a success? Typically, we listen to other people, a class of person least well placed to judge how we feel about ourselves. True success, however, is about our own lives and how we relate to them. And of course our lives will have their moments of certainty and then moments of great doubt. It is fear that we have to fight. Louis Kronenberger, the twentieth-century American critic, wrote, "We are neurotically haunted today by the imminence, and by the ignominy, of failure. We know how frightening is the cost of success and to fail is something too awful to think about." We fear failure only because we do not understand failure.

In our lives we often feel off-target and the need to make numerous corrections in order to stay on course. When we deviate off course in our lives it may seem as if we are failing. It is however no such thing, these deviations are merely part of our life's course. It is, as a result of these deviations, far easier to recognize the surge that we get from being in the right place at the right time than we know what it feels like to have been off course at the wrong time. Don't worry if sometimes things don't work out, just make the necessary corrections and get on with the business of living. You have not failed just because a few, or even a lot of things, have gone wrong. Take heart from the words of Buckminster Fuller, the American architect and thinker, "Failure is a word invented by idiots, nothing fails in nature." Many disappointments and apparent failures aren't really failures or even disappointments, very often they were just meant to happen that way.

Worrying about apparent failure will only ensure that they multiply and with time turn into the sort of failures that seriously affect your life. Failures that are self-inflicted lead to a general state of unhappiness. The strongest people do not mind losing, and so even when they lose, they seem to win. Try to like the word "no;" it can be much more instructive than "yes." A baby will probably hear the word a lot. At first the word "no" doesn't stop a baby; disregarding it, and determined to please herself, she continues. Yet, in adult life, even a whispered "no" can deter someone—make them lose heart, they take it too personally. It may not be a direct hit towards you, it may be the other person's reticence or frustration.

The word "no" can be seen as an obstacle to make you more focused. "No" may obstruct your immediate goal, but it may also turn to "maybe" and then "yes." A definite "maybe," if it is prolonged, however, is a killer—giving false hope. But if you are brave enough to push ahead you will eventually seize the truth whichever way it goes and a final answer allows you to move away or to move forward. It takes a lot of guts to reject a rejection—it is unbelievably attractive in its bravery, but if you are still rejected, in your dignity you will carry with you the knowledge that you tried as hard as possible.

People who realize a disappointment, and who do not relinquish their dreams from becoming realities, are classified as rebound personalities—they don't see failure as a defeat. Perhaps their greatest advantage is that they are clear that their failure is not personal failure. It is simply a mistake, an action outside of themselves, that they made. Some people think things happen to them, some people think they happen to the world. Rebound characters are relentless, and if you want to be successful just watch what a successful person does. If you need advice on how to succeed, ask someone who has failed, for to fail is the best way to learn how to succeed. A person who is an apparent success will not really know how they have succeeded. One who has failed will have thought long and hard about that failure. If you need to know how a clock works, take it apart. It is the same way with success and failure. You need to know what is inside, what caused the mistakes to happen. Failure is only a measure on a scale set by your contemporaries. It can be a gift—the type that your best friend will rarely have the courage to point out to you.

Sportsmen are among the best examples of turning a defeat into a triumph. In competitive sports, failure is seen as a challenge. In losing the game, the competitor will take stock of it, analyzing what went wrong, how to improve. They tend not to look back so much when they win. The more you practice, the luckier you get. One is always more vexed at losing a game of any sort by a single hole or ace than if one never had a chance of winning. "What the mind does not know about, the heart does not grieve for," is another old saying. As far as our society is concerned, success is to do something that everyone else imagines that you cannot do. It is the desire to impress that drives people on, that is sure; what is less sure, however, is whether people thus driven will find happiness and contentment. This is the dilemma that besets our lives.

Failure is just a way of describing the results you did not want, so redirect your efforts. Some say there is no such thing as failure, only feedback, or a result you did not envisage. They are outcomes rather than problems. Optimists are high achievers on the playing fields, in health and at work. Positive thought apparently improves molecular activity and endorphins in our physiology. A resilient attitude means they engage more actively with everyday life because they believe their endeavours will reap rewards. Pessimists give up easily, predict disaster, which squashes their energy, making it extremely hard for them to cold call. They refer to themselves as realists yet they cause inaction.

There are two sorts of achievements, those motivated by hopes of success and those motivated by failure. The first depends on a quest for excellence, which is healthy and mature. The second is more pathological and immature. Much of the psychology of military incompetence stems from selecting senior commanders for their physical, not moral, bravery, resulting in characters in high command positions that they may be unfit to hold. Evidently people who fear failure prefer practice and games to real living. They may gain less but they also lose less. These types also like privacy and secrecy, not open-play offices. Pure fear-based personalities try to select subordinates they consider inferior to themselves so they seem better than they really ever can be.

Early in life people are often told they are not good enough, that they will never succeed. Brush aside all negative comments and decide for yourself to focus on something better. Later in life people tend to regret not being braver or pushing themselves more, reflecting on how things could have been.

This is a total waste of effort, for water that has gone under the mill, grinds no corn. Winston Churchill said success in life consists of going from one mistake to the next without losing enthusiasm. The true art of success is learning how to cope with failure, and understanding its enlightening rewards. According to Churchill, "Approach the great chain of life one link at a time."

Happiness is making the most of yourself, making the most of your talents and accepting that you are making the most of these talents, enjoying them, and rejoicing in them. People feel regret, almost a self-disgust when they know that they have a talent they are not using. For instance, playing the piano or painting. A talent for excelling in something is seen by them as an embarrassment, so they don't get on and use that talent. Often you hear people say, "I wish that I had done this, I wish that I had done that." To expand yourself or test your talent takes courage. It is a risky business actually expanding yourself, stretching your ability and getting out of your comfort zone. In life, however, it is important to stretch your energy, for you never know how far you can go until you have gone a bit too far. It is important for your entire well being to take that challenge. Many people keep themselves down; they have the habit of diminishing themselves, putting a barbed wire fence around the possibilities of their lives. "I had better not do this, I had better not do that," an inner voice says to them, a seductive message. Risk nothing, lose nothing. When in truth the message should be risk nothing, gain nothing, and in time, lose all.

Fear of rejection is another reason why people do not take risks with their talents. Most people who have gotten somewhere in life have been rejected quite a few times. When these people are asked for advice they will say "If you want to do something, keep going, bang on the door, get used to rejection as finally the tables will turn." Oscar Wilde, the nineteenth-century playwright, poet, and novelist who wrote *The Picture of Dorian Gray*, put his pen on it when he wrote: "It's not enough just to succeed, it needs you first to fail to make success worthwhile."

People who are generally scared of making fools of themselves follow the safety-first rules and lose nothing. This safety-first policy does not work. It saps the spirit of a person, turning it from something good into a shrivelled parody of itself. If you take courage and risks with your natural ability, you will surprise yourself. Of course you will do something that is a bit foolish from time to time, but at least you will have done something. People keep themselves small only because they believe they can handle small situations and in being able to handle something, they will be happy. In fact the reverse is true: If they expand themselves beyond their perceived possibilities, the excitement, the pleasure, and the sense of achievement will be colossal.

Constantly check how you react internally and to the outside world, because your internal attitude will reflect your external delivery. Every day simple things create enjoyment, so try to deal with the smallest problems first, gaining a sense of achievement so you have the enthusiasm and dedication to overcome a more complex equation. If there is something you really want, you need to crave it every day. It is well documented how many well-known people have pinned up a photo of a hero or actress on their wall and years later realized their dreams came true in connection with that hero by training the mind to focus on desire.

There are, however, certain rules that can help us avoid real failure and achieve real success. Never refuse help, whatever your problems are, large or small, as everybody will have problems regardless of how successful and self-assured they may seem. Everyone can, from time to time, use help. The important thing is to realize that you need help. Perhaps most importantly, when you receive help, receive that help gracefully. Help however does not include advice. The old adage, that free advice is worthless, is endlessly true. Advice is a matter of opinion and may not be correct. The person who gives advice may not know all the facts. Facts are often fiction, when you have to solve a problem. Advice based on incorrect facts may be bad advice. Never ask for advice when what you need is help. To confuse advice and help only muddles the situation that you find yourself in. Always be scrupulous about repaying help and never forget the person who has helped you. If someone has helped you, that person is the right person to ask for help a second time. Do not ask for help from someone whom you have helped; one of the reasons that people are graceless when they receive help is because they imagine that if you help them then one day they will have to help you.

Apparent success comes at different moments in your life. Seldom is success spread evenly across a career. So often it appears that youth is wasted on the young. At the beginning of life, there is innocence and energy; at the end of life, experience and lethargy. Life has a distinct pattern to it, with a beginning, a middle, and an end. The beginning and the end are remarkably similar, each with a childlike quality. The middle is the part with the problems. When success or recognition of your talents comes early, there is disappointment that in the next phase these talents are not greater. This seems like failure when in fact we should be celebrating former success. Many old people look back on their lives and contemplate a history of failure. They indulge in sadness rather than celebrating the triumph of having lived. These people dwell on the mistakes, the apparent failure rather than the success of dealing with their problems; they live in a world of what might have been, rather than the real world of having made a success of dealing with the problem. They measure their own efforts against the efforts of others, rather than question themselves as to how hard they tried, if they were honest and kind, whether they had generosity of spirit, or if their life was honorable. Sophocles wrote in 409 B.C. that he would prefer even to fail without honor than win by cheating. The feeling of his sentiment is right, but the conclusion wrong. For if you act with honor, you will not fail. Failures in these essential ingredients of life need to be redeemed straight away. When you realize that you are being dishonest, or ungenerous, then you must change at once. To decide that you will change is not good enough; you must take action, not "repent at leisure." Only by changing our ways and rejecting the easier way that involves the bad characteristics of human existence can we have any chance of true success.

Happily, it is the greatest human right for all of us to be able to repent. Equally it is the greatest human right for all of us to forgive, and only in this way can failures become triumphs. From a platform of forgiveness, you can create a clarity and vision of your life that is compatible with happiness. It is the simple people who have lived kind, honorable lives who are the true heroes of everyday life. The true heroes of life are not those with pages of achievement in reference books or billions in the bank; they are simply people who come to terms with those who surround them. They are the heroes of everyday life.

Never be ashamed of apparent failure, for there is always a silver lining in every event that goes wrong. So often in literature and the cinema the apparent failure is shown as the ultimate hero. Humphrey Bogart's character Rick in *Casablanca* is a bartender who pursues apparently lost causes. He is clearly a man of talent and education in a conventional sense, however he seems to be wasting his life, and yet he is the ultimate hero. Marlon Brando's character Terry in *On the Waterfront* seems to be a down-and-out failed young boxer beaten to a pulp by Lee Cobb and his mob. Brando rises to lead the longshoremen back to work. He lost but he won. The cinema for all its fantasy portrays many human truths. While you can become downhearted with rejection, those people who reject you for the right reasons are doing you a great service. A person who is a success may become popular because of success. The people who applaud that person, however, are fickle, because the moment success fades (and it will), the admirers fade.

Often we bury our failures because we fear the sense of guilt, the stigma of failure. Hiding our failures, pretending that they are successes, will introduce a sense of falsehood into our lives. We fail to allow our failures to teach the lessons that are necessary for living. Amongst these lessons is the one on how to deal with failures. For real failure needs to be addressed and dealt with as the effects of real failure get wedged in the physiognomy of the body. If you don't understand the nature of true failure and how to come to terms with that failure, then you are taking it all too seriously and causing yourself much worry. The real problem with failure is that when it is taken too seriously it becomes self-perpetuating. You are then left with a feeling of total helplessness and incompetence, an unpleasant and often inexplicable sensation.

An acceptance of your own failure as a negative aspect of your life can create a myriad of negative feelings, anger, jealousy, hatred, and others, and eventually you may even get a strong pleasure from the guilt of failure, a feeling that you wish to repeat. It is far better that you deal with failure in a positive way and treat this strong feeling, if it should occur, as a temporary visitor, for the beauty of this strong feeling is that it will pass away. Sadly, the damage done to yourself and others by feelings of anger, jealousy, and hatred leaves scars that take time to heal.

As you should view failure in a positive light so should you view negative experiences, for they can be used as a valuable reference point later in your life, when you feel failure but are not quite sure of what the feeling means. These strong feelings may well be uncomfortable at the time, but they become a good infrastructure for your future. It is also a splendid rule of life to prepare yourself for failure and tragedy at a time when neither event is happening. You may never use the practice that you have prepared—indeed, maybe it is just because you have practiced how to deal with these situations that they do not occur. Often think of failure, play with it in your mind, make friends with the idea of failure. Never fear to fail, for failure is an integral part in the heroic nature of living.

Never worry about failure because many times failure is illusory, such as failure in a particular field set against a particular set of standards. Worry about failures of kindness and honor and honesty. Failure to succeed in a conventional sense is neither here nor there in the course of a lifetime. Often the price paid for success is such that it constitutes a failure in itself. A success achieved without honor, honesty, and kindness is a travesty leading only to a sense of suppressed unease. The secret of success, if indeed there is such a simple and singular secret, is the determination to succeed and not the determination to avoid failure. So often in life you find the very failure that you try to avoid attracted to your pathway. It is the sense of having tried to do your best with honor, honesty, and kindness that gives you a feeling of well being that is true success. It is how you handle failure that determines whether or not you succeed.

"To understand is to forgive, even yourself."

——ALEXANDER CHASE

Chapter Seven

✦

THE NEED FOR UNDERSTANDING

S O MANY OF OUR WORDS are never heard because of our own inability to listen. We use words casually and often in the wrong place at the wrong time, and as a result our lives are full of misunderstanding. In the eighteenth century Thomas Fuller wrote, "God grant me to be content with those who understand me." Communicate, we are told, otherwise relationships will break down. This is all very well, but if our communication is so distorted by a combination of emotion and sheer ignorance of the meaning of the words, then we had far better stay silent. People of Arabic origin say that some words are best swallowed. Most people, however, tend to talk colloquial rubbish and seldom say what they mean. No wonder so much of life's grief is about misunderstanding. Words are dangerous things, and if misused in desperate circumstances, they can kill.

How often have we heard the phrase from one person or another, "I say what I think," uttered with consummate pride.

How seldom do people, especially those who so pride themselves, think before speaking? How often are we asked our opinions when in truth the ones who asked us wish to hear their own opinions? When asked to give an opinion, only give one if you know about the subject on which you are questioned. Never be afraid to say that you do not know. Too often people waffle when they don't know, which only adds to the general confusion. Using language as a form of communication only works if we take care of how to use its words. Serial misunderstandings drive people apart. The aspect of that which is quite clear is the importance of the way we use words. Leaders in our world, both past and present, and for that matter future, are people who understand how to use words. They are people capable of deep and important thought, but it is the way that they deliver their thoughts that count.

Disasters come from misunderstanding words. The charge of the Light Brigade at Balaclava was a prime example. The order told the cavalry to advance and take the guns. The guns referred to were not those that the cavalry charged. This disaster had all the ingredients of the classic miscommunication. It was an order spoken by Lord Raglan, written by his adjutant, delivered by an over-enthusiastic officer to Lord Lucan, Lord Raglan's brother-in-law. The two hated each other and were perpetually quarrelling. Lord Raglan could see a set of British guns just captured by the Russians, while Lord Lucan who commanded the Light Brigade could only see Russian guns at the end of a heavily guarded valley. The order, in the context of these two officers, seemed stupid, but given their dislike for each other, no rational discussion on what appeared to be a seriously ridiculous order took place. Lord Lucan merely passed on the order and told Lord Cardigan to obey its contents. The Light Brigade charged the Russian guns, a massacre followed and debate as to who was to blame has continued ever since. In another example, when consulting the oracle at Delphi a king was told, "A great battle will be won." He understood the words, but they were deliberately misleading, for he assumed that the victory was his. In the event a great battle was won, but by the other side. Oracles know how to use words to deceive and to mislead the unwary.

Successful people, whether they are political, business, religious, or military leaders, are people who as they write and as they speak know the exact word to convey both the meaning and the emotion. Their language is simple and understandable. Scientists, who are undeniably clever but use terminology such as "enfolding" and "infolding," are unlikely to become leaders for it is hard for the population to have the remotest idea of what they mean when they speak. They have a different view of life, a very important and interesting view, which, because of their language, is largely comprehensible only to their colleagues. An exception to this rule is Margaret Thatcher, a practicing scientist, who went on to be the first scientist to govern a nation, excluding Thomas Jefferson, President of the United States of America. Still, Margaret Thatcher's background as a scientist colored her use of language. Her statement, for example, that "there is no such thing as Society" enraged the left of the British political spectrum. Margaret Thatcher the scientist thought that there was no such thing as a collective state, rather a state made up of many constituent parts, much as air or water, a formula, or collection of parts that together form an element.

There is an optimism about science, from the Middle Ages when they believed that they could turn base metal into gold with the right mixture of constituent parts, to modern day dreams of getting a man on the moon, where scientists believed the right mixture of technology would succeed. How strange it is that the discipline that takes the greatest account of the meaning of a word be the one least able to express itself in terms that most people can understand. The lesson is clear: words must mean what you mean them to mean. But this, however, is not enough because we have conversations with each other on many levels.

Words must combine with the body language of emotion to convey a message. Often in conversation we agree, while privately we think, "I don't agree with that one bit." We leave that conversation feeling a bit down and depressed that we allowed something that was manifestly wrong to pass unchallenged. Don't worry about this, let it pass, ride with the mood and wait for the mood to change. You can waste so much time correcting the misconceptions of others. For the most part their ideas and false facts are irrelevant to you. It is all a matter of judgement of where to fight and where to retreat, a judgement made all the harder by this depressing feeling as you walk away from conflict. Don't worry about it. There are times when you feel depressed, not on the top of your form, but don't let it get you down. You may have to go further than you imagine with a mood sparked by avoiding verbal conflict. Imagine yourself in a dark alley, there seems nowhere to go but down this narrow alleyway. (Do not despair; hopeless moments are really quite special. You just have to get through one to realize this.) In time when you look back, it is these dark moments that are often the most exciting. It is not just the light at the end of the tunnel that pulls you forward, it is also the light behind you that drives you on.

Most of us who work, do so with other people, whether we are seeing them in some way, looking after them, caring for them, talking about the day's business with them, or working alongside them in the same organization. It's quite common in a workforce for a hate situation to develop whereby one or more people are particularly disliked. For an employer not to spot a victim amongst the workforce is unfortunate; for the employer to select the victim, which is often the case, is criminal. Usually when you ask why someone does not like someone else they will reply, "They're just not my type of person." This is a meaningless phrase, for in fact the persons concerned are more likely to be similar than different, or they would not have graduated to similar jobs in the same organization in the same part of the country.

André Gide wrote in August, 1921, "Each of us understands in others only those feelings he is capable of producing himself." In this case, two people recognize their similarities and dislike each other for them, immediately digesting an impression of a colleague's personality and disliking him or her as a matter of principal with the casual words, "They're not my cup of tea," and building up a continuing dislike of that person. To come to terms with the personality of others needs work. In Mark Twain's words, one learns people through the heart, not the eyes or the intellect.

Ralph Waldo Emerson concluded in 1842 that all persons are puzzles until at last we find in some word or act the key to the man or to the woman. Stephen Covey, in his highly successful book, *The Seven Habits of Highly Effective People*, writes, "You can always seek first to understand. That's something that's within your control. And as you do that, as you focus on your circle of influence, you really, deeply understand other people, you have accurate information to work with, you get to the heart of matter quickly, you build emotional bank accounts, and you give people the psychological air that they need so you can work together effectively."

Words are important in the process of people coming to terms with each other. The right word binds, the wrong word divides. It is, however, a hard enough judgement to choose the right words without the added hazard that the words may have a meaning you did not intend. A happy workforce is an articulate workforce where workers talk to each other, where understanding flourishes, and where misunderstanding can therefore be overcome. Whether the company flourishes or not will have some effect on the happiness of its workforce. Happiness comes from the relationships with one another in the workplace, whether it be camaraderie in adversity, or pride in achievement. Whether the company flourishes will be directly dependent on whether the workforce is happy. The point of communication is to understand what you are saying and to understand how the message will be understood. If the message is not understood, the fault lies clearly with the sender, not with the receiver.

Amongst the most cunning of words is the use of flattery. To quote Oscar Wilde, "One who doubts the power of flattery clearly never has been flattered." Flattery is the infantry of negotiation. Flattery has a bad name, unjustifiably, as flattery is useful to both the flatterer and the one flattered. We often find it hard to receive flattery and reject flattery in a gauche manner. Practice receiving flattery because it makes you feel better and there is no real harm done. Flattery is easy to spot. The statement, "You look beautiful today," may well be true but also counts as flattery. "Your hair style is awful" is clearly meant to be a truthful observation, yet it counts as a deadly insult.

When using words it is important to take the culture of a person into account. In the East, truth is important; in the West, politeness supersedes truth. Today the world is accessible almost in its entirety. Populations have moved, entwined, changed their habits, and brought their languages with them. All this is a good reason to be particularly careful in the use of words. Habits are in the blood, or as some will say, the spirit. Habits that are thousands of years old are passed down to us by people of whose existence we are barely aware. Habits shape our acceptable vocabulary, and how we react to the vocabulary of others. The aboriginal Gadarcha men and their witch doctors decide that a member of theirs or some other tribe should die. To kill them they leave certain symbols in the way of that person, then that person deciphers these symbols and upon understanding, dies.

We seldom understand the real nature of reality, such as changes in relationships, and when we do we communicate reality. It is typically in such an obtuse fashion that what is intended as help becomes a hindrance. In a search for happiness you have to watch out for reality, and when you recognize it, reveal it in as simple and understandable way as is possible. Never fear reality, for it is better that you tell the truth about yourself than another tells lies about your truth. The forbidden aspect of our own reality is something that we hide, though it is better to reveal that forbidden reality and let others make their own judgements based on our truth. Living with a hidden secret will bring the unhappiness of fear. In the end those that like and love us will continue to do so, those that dislike us will simply say, "I always knew that they were a bad lot." Tennessee Williams, the American playwright who wrote *Cat on a Hot Tin Roof,* understood this when he wrote, "I don't ask for your pity, but just your understanding. Not even that, but just your recognition of me in you, and Time, the enemy in us all."

To improve is one of the strongest human instincts. We try to improve each other endlessly; that is what advice really is, the desire of one person to improve another, living vicariously through someone else's life. Before giving advice, however, we need to consider our ability to recommend an alteration; and here lies the biggest misunderstanding of all. We believe that we are competent to plan the lives of others. Indeed, if we were clones, then this would not only be true but sensible. We are, however, all irreconcilably different and that is the wonder of our world. Few people, however, realize this. W.E.B. DuBois, the first African American to receive a Ph.D. from Harvard University and a great scholar and defender of the Afro-Americans, wrote in 1903, "Herein lies the tragedy of the age: not that men are poor,—all men know something of poverty; not that men are wicked,—who is good? Not that men are ignorant,—what is Truth? Nay, but that men know so little of men." Only when we realize this are we capable of happiness.

Understanding can be an unexpected and sudden event. The smile from a stranger has immense beauty; it is an intimate yet fleeting movement, never to be repeated. It is a symbol of good will passing between two people. Perversely, the easiest way to be warm is to open your heart to others, an easy suggestion to write, a very hard action to take. In the first place, it is emotionally expensive to be warm and open. People have the perception that in doing this they will lose, get hurt, be made a fool of, for most of us have hearts patched with Scotch tape. We are inclined to feel both that our needs have not been truly met and that the easiest way to get our needs met is to do it ourselves. To do this in isolation and independence, however, is not the real answer, for we desperately need the reactions that we get from others. So how shall we treat others to avoid the misunderstandings that lurk like landmines in our lives? The answer is to connect with other people appropriately, to be warm and reinforcing, caring and honest.

The Chinese say the heart is the supreme sovereign and all the other organs are known as the officials, but the heart governs the overall spirit of a person. Unlike Western medicine, Chinese medicine is used to find the root cause of symptoms as well as eliminating symptoms. Underneath the surface you will find that a manipulator is not a really happy person—he may have highs when his constant manoeuvres pay quick dividends but he will have lows with new schemes to keep others in the dark and at bay. Putting that much ambition as a priority before liking someone or caring about a valuable friendship will eventually harm the spirit of the heart and cause distress. To stop a conflict, try not to blame someone. Instead of being certain they are wrong, show a curiosity. Through this curiosity you may enlarge your perspective and be less certain of your righteousness—in your story versus their story, give their story a chance. Alexander Chase wrote in 1966, "to understand is to forgive," and added more importantly, "even yourself."

"Each man has only one genuine vocation, to find the way to himself," according to Herman Hesse, the twentieth-century Nobel-prize winning novelist and poet. This can be even harder in our complex technological age. Forward thinking retailer and philanthropist, Edward Filene, spoke in 1935, "There is no eternal principle more definitely established than the principle of constant change." Nearly seventy years later there is only one enormous change to this statement, which is the speed of change itself is changing, and accelerating. People need to decipher faster than ever the flood of information of changes, so-called "about to happens," that may or may not materialize.

Other people's intentions are often hidden. This is because thoughts are invisible and the thoughts are in their brains not ours. G.K. Chesterton, the twentieth-century British writer, understood the potential purpose of understanding others: "If you do not understand a man you cannot crush him," and then the reality of the situation, "and if you do understand him, you probably will not crush him." If you put a person in a position where they have to defend themselves, you are not trusting their intentions. Avoidance is another overused tactic. Far better to contribute how you experienced an incident then avoid telling the person how you reacted. Underneath it all, most people can tell a truth told from the heart and can then react calmly. If it is a carefully articulated truth they will be far less distressed by it then if it comes from a heated head.

Reputation is everything. Once lost it is seldom regained. A reputation can take a lifetime to build and be lost in a minute. Napoleon was conscious of his reputation: "A great reputation is a great noise, the more that there is of it the further does it swell, land, monuments, nations all fall but the noise remains, and will reach to other generations." He was right, of course, for he lost land, monuments, and nations. His reputation has, however, resounded down the generations, and the noise of it still buffets history and forever grows.

"The possible's slow fuse is lit by the imagination."

——EMILY DICKINSON

Chapter Eight

Chapter Eight

RETURN ON
IMAGINATION

L IFE BREAKS DOWN into plodding and inspired thoughts. Every single building, film, book, dress, recipe, starts with a thought, and thought really starts in the imagination. One of the most important aspects of a child's development is to encourage imagination. To be really effective your imagination must run ahead of reality. Imagining the seemingly impossible makes it possible. Our minds create our futures and therefore our realities. Many people get through life by slogging away at objectives without any real thought as to what these objectives should be or how they should be achieved. The people who are really successful identify objectives and then use their imaginative qualities to get there.

Imaginative people operate on many levels simultaneously, whereas less creative people operate on a mono level. With the first group it is a quirky thought of one individual that triggers the inventiveness of the rest. A quirky thought from one person leads to embellishment by another followed by an even more absurd thought that ultimately triggers the ridiculous. In recollection we have access to our past, in imagination we have access to our future, yet we use the materials of our past to invent the possibilities of our future. "Imagination is the secret and morrow of civilization. It is the very eye of pith," wrote Henry Ward Beecher in 1887 in his book, *Proverbs from Plymouth Pulpit*. These proverbs were as true then for society as they are today for business, where the words "it is the eye of the pith" should be replaced with "it is the eye of the business." Imagination, when applied to business, shows the way to success. And for imagination to work in business it must work at all levels.

Percy Shaw's inspiration for a roadside design in 1933 that saved thousands of lives came from observing real cats' eyes glinting in the fog as he drove home. The design involved fixing a spherical lens into a rubber pad set in iron and embedded in the middle of the road that helped drivers to stay in the correct lanes. The paper clip is an even simpler piece of genius. Johan Vaaler patented a thin piece of steel wire bent into a double oval in 1901. Still in massive use a century later, the paper clip can be undone and used to mend a watch, as a shoe lace, as a bookmarker, to unclog a pepper mill amongst many other imaginative options. The very concept of imagination allows it to be utilized at many job levels.

Emily Dickinson wrote in 1862, "The possible's slow fuse is lit by the imagination." Imagination leads to invention whether that be in business or in private life, but it is also true that imagination is a far greater force in life than mere invention. Joseph

Conrad, Poland-born, British author of *Heart of Darkness* and *Lord Jim*, got it right in 1912 when he wrote these words: "Only in men's imagination does every truth find an effective and undeniable existence. Imagination, not invention, is the supreme master of art as of life." Probably in these short sentences Joseph Conrad came closer to the secret of life than many men considered far wiser than he. Imagination does in fact spread farther than the workplace, and this is why it is so important to employ imaginative people and to show imagination in the people that you employ. An employee who is imaginative in his or her private life will be more effective at work and exactly the same goes for employers.

John F. Kennedy, arguably one of America's most imaginative presidents, said in an address during 1963, "The problems of the world cannot possibly be solved by sceptics or cynics whose horizons are limited by the obvious realities. We need people who dream of things that never were." Despite these encouraging words, true success of imagination comes from its companion, discipline. It is the combination of discipline and imagination that brings about success. A person of great imagination cannot bring about a success just with ideas. He or she must sit down and put these ideas in a point, the thought is not enough. So it is with the writer. Great thoughts in the head need to be put on paper. Discipline is at least half of the masterpiece.

To fully deploy your imagination, it is important to be relaxed and detached and at ease. This is a difficult state to reach for many busy professionals and even more difficult to distinguish. Relaxing does not simply come from a change of routine, or a family holiday that can be incredibly nerve-wracking. In fact, the Christmas period has the highest amount of heart attacks and divorces of any time of the year, and it takes most people till the spring to recover from Christmas. It is helpful in practicing your imagination to work and live amongst people who understand and appreciate imagination.

People with a lack of imagination become tense and their lives so structured that any variation causes them colossal stress. Even thinking about a variation to them would be stressful. Try going to an airport and changing your destination at the last moment. An impossible idea? Of course not, only one that needs imagination and courage to carry out. An idea that when implemented will give an enormous sense of release that is relaxation. A lot of people hover through life without the imagination to do something different and the courage to implement that imagination. They live in fear of the novel and terror of the unexpected. It is not necessary for this to be the case. However, surprisingly few conduct their lives in a decisive and imaginative way.

Relaxing also comes from cultivating and concentrating on your memories. Emerson wrote in 1860, "There are no days in life so memorable as those which vibrated to some stroke of the imagination." A lot of people don't have memories. This is sadly the case if there has been trauma in childhood and the child has had to shut out the memory in order to survive. Equally, someone will have a negative incident from the past that they continually replay. It is no good continually thinking about regaining the negative events of your life. Put away most occurrences or thoughts that you can't do anything about. You need positivity to move forward. Memory without imagination is a poor thing. Regression therapy can be a tremendous help working through past traumas but it needs to be approached with great caution—it is in the category of rebirthing, a practice to be thought about carefully before you set out doing that path. Try hard to forget the hurt in the past and, if this is not possible, remember that forgiveness gets the problem resolved in your own mind. If you can do nothing about the negative memory in question just accept that and put the memories to one side. Get rid of all negativity and use your imagination to fill your mind with positive thoughts.

All of us have a private cinema in our minds. We often play edited moments of our lives on our private mental cinema screen. This is highly beneficial to our general well being and poignant as the lovely ones bring us tremendous joy. Most of us are a lot more creative than we give ourselves credit and we give ourselves low marks in this area. The ability of the brain to link one object with another in ever-expanding ways is staggering and ought to be taught in schools to greater effect. A rigidly taught mind will try to think sensibly, but a broadly taught mind will try to break traditional boundaries.

Discipline is necessary to turn imagination into its own reality. Without the first quality the second is an empty void, a thing of little real value except in the carrying out of the mindless actions. After imagination and discipline comes curiosity and enthusiasm, courses that should be part of the national curriculum but aren't taught in school, for to acquire these traits will be a lifetime of learning. Of the four qualities of a balanced life only one is part of the Western education system. Not surprisingly, discipline, taught on its own, is falling into disrepute. Teachers are reluctant for a myriad of reasons to teach this virtue. It is hard for a teacher to teach imagination in a formal sense because imagination is by its very nature novel while teaching is, equally by its nature, repetitive. It follows therefore that what should be taught is the value of imagination.

Take, for example, the dyslexic pupil. Special schools and special colleges are set up to help dyslexic children conform to a system. Dyslexia gives the greatest talent any child can have, an amazing imagination. An amazing imagination that should be valued and developed, not changed and reshaped to pass exams meant for less gifted children. Luckily the teaching profession realized that dyslexia existed. Previously, generations of children have been dismissed as low achievers, put to one side, and ignored in a class filled with apparently "clever" children.

Andrew Carnegie, the great American entrepreneur and industrialist, once said: "It takes a good mind to survive an education." What he really meant was that a whole range of people who were neglected by the education system has succeeded in artistic and unconventional areas, whereas those with a traditional education failed. The imaginative mind rejects monotony, the trained mind accepts monotony. Each year students are fresh and the teacher knows full well that he or she has to teach the same things once again. Naturally, a bored teacher will gravitate towards a naturally clever pupil. It is more interesting to teach someone who simply understands what you are saying and will pass exams than someone who is likely to fail. The education system of the Western world is geared towards passing exams. Facts are the most important aspect of education, when imagination is not considered. We have referred before to Einstein, a man who regularly failed exams but became one of the most important scientists of the twentieth century. A dyslexic, he was hopeless at school exams but brilliantly imaginative. An Irish industrialist, Ted Power, the founder of Murphy Television and Radio, asked Einstein how he went about discovering his theory of relativity. Power, a man of extraordinary imagination, asked him, "Did you go A. B. C. D. and afterwards, fill in the missing parts?". "Yes," was Einstein's reply.

A sense of the absurd is the most sophisticated sense of humor; it makes life far less painful for those that have this kind of mind set. Life throws so many absurdities into your path, it is necessary to recognize them for what they are, to laugh and carry on with being. A sense of the absurd is a subtle yet simple thing. It is, in fact, the ability to see humor in everyday situations. The greatest humor comes from the mundane and obvious mixed with a huge dose of imagination. It is a humor detected by instinct from the madness, humor found in what we do, the humor found in what we think. It is impossible to have a sense of the absurd without imagination, for the humor of the absurd largely comes from taking these everyday actions and extending them in our minds to the point where they become absurd and make us laugh. How often we have heard the words, if you didn't laugh, it would make you cry. Humor helps make life bearable, mitigates sadness, encourages joy, and takes the sting out of a bad situation.

Yet, humor without imagination is the dull repetition of other people's jokes delivered with monotonous regularity; it is torture inflicted on a captive audience. The development of the imagination is not always easy; reality is often pressing too hard on us for imagination to subdue uneasy thoughts.

Imagination gives the sense of the ridiculous that is the antidote to pomposity. Imagination is about being a multi-millionaire while on your way to visit your bank manager to ask for a loan to buy a modest car. Imagination is a world without a shred of reality. According to the British playwright and novelist Somerset Maugham, in 1938, "Imagination grows by exercise, and contrary to common belief, is more powerful in the mature than in the young." It is, however strangely, imagination that will shape the world that we will live in during the next decade. Imagination can be summed up in the old joke of a group of architects sitting down to design a house and ending up with a camel. A more ungainly creature you would be hard pushed to find, but a brilliant tool given the right environment, such as to move freight in the desert.

Imagination entertains us and imagination frightens us. We find imaginative people disturbing and search out the banal to reassure us. We often feel guilty about our imagination, believing that it is self-indulgence, which is why when our brains are tired and we are not thinking too hard, good ideas just pop up. Imagination is no use without courage. On its own, imagination becomes an escape from reality. Applied with courage, however, it is really imagination that becomes the solution to our problems. Imagining the seemingly impossible makes it seem possible. And if we do not achieve all that we imagine, then at least we will achieve some of what we imagine rather than going nowhere. The very act of achieving something will make us feel better about ourselves. Our minds plan our futures and therefore our realities. Many people struggle to get through their lives by slogging away at vague objectives without any real idea as to what these objectives really are and why they need them. The people who are really successful identify objectives that may seem improbable given the person's time and circumstances. Still successful people use their imaginative qualities to achieve their imagined ambitions.

"That which we know is but little; that which we have a presentiment of is immense; it is in this direction that the poet outruns the learned man," wrote Joseph Roux in 1886 in his book *Meditations of a Parish Priest*. He suggests that those with knowledge look down on those with imagination, which is largely true. He points out, however, that the imaginative man can beat the learned man, for it is innovation that will win every time over convention. Albert Einstein said, "The mind is for thinking with, not remembering." Facts are easy to find, so there is little point in rendering them, as they can be quickly looked up. Imagination is perhaps the greatest gift. However, as with all gifts, the joy comes when you have learned how to appreciate them. It is folly to neglect imagination, for imagination needs maintenance, hard work, and plenty of practice. Your imagination needs taking care of, but that care returns rewards a billion fold, more than the effort needed to keep an imagination in good repair.

*"Success is counted sweetest, by those who
have never succeeded."*

——EMILY DICKINSON

Chapter Nine

✒

UNDERSTANDING
SUCCESS

I T IS VITAL TO HEAR famous people's thoughts on success because they have in fact experienced the nature of success and were naturally successful. For example, the twentieth-century eminent British philosopher, Bertrand Russell, wrote, "Unless a man has been taught what to do with success after getting it, the achievement of it must inevitably leave him prey to boredom." For centuries, success and the achieving of it has been the aim of mankind yet, once found, was of little real value. Success is not achievement, according to Ambrose Bierce, the American satiric writer and author of *The Devil's Dictionary*. In the nineteenth century, Bierce defined achievement in his dictionary as "The Death of Endeavour and the Birth of Disgust."

Oscar Wilde, the English nineteenth-century writer and poet, was a man who knew both success and failure. He was often quoted for the simple reason that he invented most of the really good quotes. Wilde was, in this respect, a success, quoted because he is worth quoting—a rare case of ability equalling fame. In one of his more memorable quotes, however, he wrote, "Success is entirely due to luck, ask any failure." Not only is this statement extremely witty, but also it has the essential aspect that sets it apart from statements that are merely clever. Oscar Wilde has got at the very nature of success, which is the impossibility of really accessing what is in truth successful. Businesses rising from nothing are hailed as great successes and then as great failures. People who to the world seem to be successful often feel total failures. So, in search for success and its true nature, let us first examine luck.

A person's luck is judged on appearances—he is a lucky person, the other is an unlucky person. Nevertheless, luck comes in pieces. You are never wholly lucky or, for that matter, wholly unlucky. In truth, luck cannot be relied upon to deliver success anymore than success can be relied upon to deliver happiness. Machiavelli, a considerable student of the human condition, wrote of luck or, in his words, fortune. His words, written five hundred years ago, are as true today as they were true then:

> "I compare [luck] to one of these raging rivers which when in flood overflows the plains, sweeping away trees and buildings, bearing away soil from place to place, everything flies before it. So it happens with fortune who shows her power where valour has not prepared to resist her, and thither she turns her forces where she knows that barriers of defence have not been raised to restrain her."

In a rather shorter statement, a famous American golfer uttered the same sentiments—"The more I practice the luckier I get." How do companies move from good to great results—not by a miracle formula, not through a crisis wake-up call, but by consistent down to earth hard work and a commitment to excellence and people. Leaders of great companies do not start out by deciding where they are going, but with whom. They focus on the people first, and they let the wrong people off the bus before they start the journey.

Frederick the Great was of the view that the older one gets, the more convinced one becomes that "His Majesty King Luck does three quarters of the business of this miserable world." Machiavelli, on the other hand, takes a middle course in his splendid book on human nature, *The Prince*: "I hold it to be true that fortune is the arbiter of one half of our actions." Nowhere in the entire work does Machiavelli predict the downfall of a state or ruler or, for that matter, even a contemporary general. Unlike Nostradamus and many others who have predicted entire events, even the end of the world, Machiavelli confines himself in his book almost entirely to an understanding of the circumstances of mankind. He is right, of course, for it does not matter whether you are engaged in ruling a nation, fighting a war, running a business, or merely trying to get through a humdrum life as best as you can; the first principal to understand is the importance of human nature.

Humans come in all shapes and sizes and so it is with their natural intelligence. Machiavelli understood this as he also understood how people behaved in the myriad of different circumstances in which they found themselves. Success is due to effort but not the sort of effort that we generally associate with what we normally take to be success. Charles Dudley Warner, the nineteenth-century American editor and author, put his pen on the dilemma of success when he wrote in 1873, "I know that unremitting attention to business is the price of success but I don't know what success is."

The key to successful leadership is to get to know your style. Success, both in the material and the true sense, is largely dependent on people and it is therefore advisable to learn sensitivity. Real success does not come from holding yourself from others but rather from working to understand them, knowing the reasons why they take particular attitudes. Real success comes from understanding a person's shortcomings and finding as much joy in their shortcomings as in their advantages.

History shows, however, that the men and women whom we now regard as great geniuses were considered out of step with their times. These people were seldom successful during their lives. Machiavelli himself was exiled, imprisoned, tortured, and reviled. His greatest work was only published many years after his death. *The Prince* has been both praised and reviled ever since. Machiavelli understood only too well what motivated people: namely, the glory of riches. People today are as interested in these material and social benefits as they were in Machiavelli's days, but are these outward signs really the signs of a true success? Machiavelli is quite clear on the matter of luck and skill:

For my part I consider that it is better to be adventurous than cautious because fortune is a woman, and if you wish to keep her under it is necessary to beat and ill use her, and it is seen that she allows herself to be mastered by the adventurous rather than by those who go to work more coldly, she is therefore always woman-like, a lover of young men because they are less cautious, more violent and with more audacity command her.

Failure or success in business is in the end up to you; how you behave is all important. Forget about luck, it will come and go with its own certainty in its own time and place. Set about your business affairs with a determination to achieve success, rather than a determination to avoid failure. The trick, however, is to transfer a business success into making a success of living. It is ironic to consider that a business success could be the first piece of bad luck that you ever have had. The acid test for success in living is not the test that others apply to your life. For others, wealth is important—private jets, yachts, a multiplicity of homes. How their homes are decorated and, more important, who decorated them. Making money blends into and then dominates your social life.

With money comes power and the social position. In America success is judged by money, in England by rank, in France by intellect. Each of these, admirable in their own way, becomes an advantage or disadvantage depending on how you acquired these goals. For the one who would be successful in living, the acid test comes in those few moments before you fall asleep at night; do you smile gently? As you fall asleep are you at one with yourself? This is the moment of truth. Many people, however, who achieve material success along the way acquire the ability of self-deception. To begin with, they deceive others and in time they deceive themselves. In the moment before sleep they think of tomorrow, forgetting the shortcomings of their behaviour on that day.

Honor in business is as paramount as it is in life. You cannot be honorable when it is convenient and dishonorable when honor will be inconvenient. The same is true of fairness: there is no halfway house, you either are fair or unfair. How you order your life in these respects is not an à la carte menu. In all of us there is good and evil to some degree. It is the circumstances that we find ourselves in that largely dictate the proportions of either the good or the evil that become apparent. Honor and fairness along with honesty are the yardsticks by which we reassure ourselves. However, people are often more prone to behaving dishonorably, unfairly, and dishonestly when events move to their disadvantage.

Obviously, dishonorable and dishonest behaviour is highly undesirable and makes real success almost an impossibility. Unfairness, also, is a habit that once acquired is hard to lose. Unfairness will affect your relationship with a series of individuals whose ill will may well hinder your commercial success, let alone your real success. An employer, for example, needs to be scrupulously fair. Criticisms should be objective, based on facts, not on hearsay and the opinions of other people who have their own agendas. These instincts are quite as important when dealing with your friends and relatives as with your employers and colleagues, for, once again, habits formed in your private life will spread over into your commercial life (and the reverse of this proposition is equally true). It is important to remember when you ask someone to perform a task for you, whether it is as an employer or a friend, that you take care to think carefully whether they are able to do what you ask. Do not get upset if they tell you that they are not capable of performing the task that you ask, for an honest friend will tell you the truth. With an employee or colleague at work, however, do not expect them to inform you that they cannot make the grade if they fail. The mistake is yours for asking them to carry out a task beyond their capability. Never blame others for your own mistakes.

Ever since the birth of Mercury, the ancient god of business, business as a name has become synonymous with sharp practice, dubious honesty, and ruthlessness. Mercury demonstrated all of these on the first day of his life, robbing both his elder brother Apollo of his cattle and then his mother. If ever a person demonstrated a talent for dishonesty, double-dealing, and sharp practice it was Mercury. While the ancient gods half hidden in the sulphuric flames of the earth's first days are works of fiction, they were born from the keen observations and writings of scholars who drew inspiration from their fellow citizens. Habits attributed to Mercury thousands of years ago were influenced by an ancient Greek distaste for business, and they have influenced how we have thought about business ever since. A stain of guilt has descended from ancient times into the subconsciousness of mankind. Aided no doubt by the ominous tones of the biblical parable of the camel having less trouble getting through the eye of the needle than a rich man's chances of getting into the kingdom of heaven, along with laws until late medieval times in Christian and Islamic societies against money lending, and later the eighteenth-century Venetian sumptuary laws which forbade conspicuous consumption, this guilt is still strongly embedded in our modern minds.

The guilt of good fortune comes to us from antiquity, with the warning that if you have good fortune, you will just as surely have bad fortune. Here at the very heart of success we have the idea that good fortune comes in a cycle coupled with bad fortune. Once again we are back at the beginning with luck; even if we do not believe in luck, we are still left with fear. In truth we fear success because we fear failure and believe that we cannot have one without the other. So it is no great wonder that we are uneasy with success. To be successful at living, then, does not entail the creation of great wealth, prestige, position, or property, but rather winning the fight against fear. How on earth can we live comfortably when our minds are filled with fear, fear of success, fear of failure? Indifference, however, is not a viable excuse to get out of searching for the path to happiness because it often masks true desire, and abnegates responsibility and accountability, thereby leading to disaster both at home and at work.

In the search for true success, it is highly important that we are diligent in how we order our work. There comes a sense of satisfaction from a job well done that gives us an inner warmth.

It does not matter whether you are a merchant, baker, or a carpenter, the perfectly fulfilled and honestly conducted task is a true success. The task in question can be a grand public task completed to the applause of those who witness that task, or it can be a small, private task where no one observes the work that has been put into that task's successful completion. For instance, the carpenter who spends as much time and effort on the quality of a cabinet's back as on the quality of that cabinet's front. Some people have it in them to seek perfection, others have in them to only go for the quick buck. The former will derive satisfaction from their work, the latter will take short cuts and cheat.

There is no quick fix to success. The ability to readjust during times of crisis is crucial in business. Many difficulties occur during times of personal adjustment, and changes are needed as a result. A company that facilitates supportive conditions and helps the inner strength of the individual will stabilize. There is the good of the individual and the good of the company. Other people connect to us in three basic ways—looking at us, speaking to us, and touching us. In the office there will be a lot less of the last one. Those that cannot connect with us in these three ways are blind, deaf, paralyzed, or perhaps, on a mental level, they have a disorder. Our senses and actions are validated by someone else's gaze, words, and touch. When the gaze is mutual we have acknowledged each other's existence and we take it in turns to speak to one another. Listening and talking is the greatest investment in any successful alliance, and even in rushed moments, it is important to give your full attention. This mutual recognition assures the most mature form of communication, interdependency, which demands aligning one's efforts with those of others and putting personal issues aside in respect to the greater cause, be it at home or at work.

To be relaxed and content one needs to achieve a sense of one's own truth, whatever shape that may be. This is what Carl Jung understood to be rigorous introspection, or inner self-examination, the ability to have an overview and self-monitor how you manage a change in circumstances. Many people who appear perfectly sane for many years can suddenly suffer loss of confidence precipitated by a small change foisted upon them—like a change of a manager at work. The paradox here is that you appear adaptable even though you are having particular difficulty accepting the change. Inside you may be filled with tension and anxiety, and as long as the pressure is not too great, the outside appearance is that you can cope. But it might only take one task involving something you do not think you can do to make you crack. This often arises from having an idealized view of what you can do—the ideal self, the gap between how we would like to be and how we see ourselves. Understand yourself and if need be, change your own picture of your role and your goal, start with the end in mind, otherwise your ladder of success may be leaning against the wrong wall.

Business can be conducted with honor, honesty, consideration, kindness, fairness, and sensitivity, and if so, these attributes will produce a sense of success. Similarly, business can be conducted on a grab-as-much-as-you-can basis without consideration for anyone except yourself. This is the choice we all have to make. Another quality that helps for business to be truly fulfilling and its success to be a true success is loyalty. Loyalty is of the utmost importance when you are assessing those whom you employ, or indeed those who would employ you, for loyalty. It is a two-way street. Loyalty commands loyalty and it must not only be given but be seen to be given. Loyalty means concern for others in sickness and health, in good times and bad times. It is essential to recognize those who are disloyal only when circumstances force them to be disloyal or whether they are individuals for whom disloyalty is part of their character. The latter persons are destructive in both their business lives and their personal lives. Loyalty comes from trust, a trust that is based on all our integrity in all our actions. Do not expect those with whom you have dealings as employees, fellow workers, or friends to put their trust in you if you do not trust them. Out of loyalty comes respect, and without respect, there can be no loyalty. If you respect others, they will respect you. Abusive language, aggressive behaviour, drunkenness, and a refusal to cooperate with others reduce the respect that others have for you and so reduce your respect for yourself.

Loyalty to friends is vital. Do not be tempted to change old friends for new friends, no matter how clever the friends appear to be. Never allow newcomers to persuade you to act against your better judgement and in particular persuade you to turn against those who have given their loyalty to you. Never shirk from your responsibilities as a friend. Never fail to express your appreciation and gratitude to others. To break any of these rules will sour your success, a personal success that has the potential to transcend the success or failure of a team or group of which you are a part.

In many ways the private success of knowing that you have played your part to the best of your ability is probably the closest that any of us will come to success. The words of Lord Haldane, a man who knew considerable public success, come as close as possible to describing private and true success. A statesman, philosopher, minister of war and Lord Chancellor of Britain, Lord Haldane wrote in his memoirs:

> The best that ordinary mortals can hope for is the result which will probably come from sustained work directed by as full a reflection as is possible. This result may be affected adversely by circumstances, by illness, by misfortune, or by death. But if we have striven to think and to do work based on thought then we have at least the sense of having striven, with such faculties as we have possessed devoted to the striving. And that is in itself a cause of happiness, going beyond the possession of any definite gain.

Lord Haldane not only captures the spirit of honor, but also the definition of honesty and sensitivity, fairness and kindness. As for luck, he suggests that it will affect us materially, but should never affect our approach to life. The person who adopts the attitude suggested by Lord Haldane is likely to be as good an employee as an employer.

There is a lack of reality about public success. First, any two people either watching an event or reading an account of that event are likely to come away with different impressions of how the people concerned in the event behaved. People well displaced towards the participants in that event will speak well of them. Those who heard of the event or even watched it, and are not well disposed to the participants, would speak badly of them. "You cannot please all people all of the time" is a great truth and, therefore, public success is flawed by its very nature. To please just one person is a far easier task with the exception of course of one's self, who is the only person you must please to be a real success. If, by nature, you are easily pleased with your own efforts, this is in itself a fair guide to the fact that you will not find true success. You must be your own sternest critic, but in being that stern critic you must apply the criteria of honesty, honor, and fairness, and, what is more, these criteria must be applied with sensitivity and fairness. In truth, public success can be a considerable disadvantage, for the simple reason that when the world says that you are doing brilliantly, there seems no reason to change. As change involves risk, why take a risk when everything in the garden is beautiful?

Change brings progress, and if we do not move forward, our minds will rest in a cozy certainty while our subconscious will gather an increasing sense of ill-ease. A sense of uncertainty will spread through us in conflict with the apparent certainty of our situation. In this public success, we have money in profusion and the adulation of an apparently adoring public, which, as it turns out, knows only our public personae. Those close to us praise us for their own gain, those who would criticize us stay silent out of fear. Fear pervades our souls, fear of rejection and fear of failure. We fear that we may be mistaken and although we do what we thought we always did well, we fear that we may still be failures. There is a theatrical saying: The clown will play Hamlet. "We have inside us the urge to break the mould to change our lives." "The grass is always greener on the other side of the fence" is another adage that expresses the urge for change that ferments in the human mind. This unease can be controlled with pills and analysts, mere palliatives for they do not get to the root of the problem. Always remember there are only three certainties in life: taxation, death, and change. With care the first of these can be avoided, but the second and third will in time have their moment.

Success to many is similar to the waiter who carries a tray of champagne glasses filled with vintage champagne through a crowded room. He must watch every move of those around him, anticipate their reactions to each other, one false move then the waiter, tray, and champagne go flying. When the same waiter carries only empty, used glasses he fears nothing and moves with confidence. Real success is when you can behave as the latter waiter while carrying the burden of the former.

Success is for the truly successful a secret thing, known only to the person concerned. And these successes, where do you find them? Amongst tycoons, entrepreneurs, bankers, or clerks, taxi drivers, and priests? The truly successful are found in all walks of life, you know them by the sense of certainty that they have as they go about their lives. In the end it is the Bible in the book of Mark chapter 8 verse 36 that poses the question fundamental to the value of success. "What shall it profit a man if he shall gain the whole world and lose his own soul?" Success must be, if it is a thing worth having, a part of your soul—a state achieved by an approach to every aspect of your life, rather than brilliance demonstrated in only one respect.

"Happiness is the ultimate revenge."

—ANONYMOUS

Chapter Ten

✍

HAPPINESS

HAPPINESS, AT ITS ROOT, is about liking yourself. Start by tolerating, then understanding yourself. First, accommodate your defeats, then raise the level by improving your behavior and care towards yourself and others. You can't be happy unless you get rid of your self-disgust. If you have a secret, ghastly habit either come to terms with it, if you won't stop it, or replace it with something more positive. Real addiction is damaging whatever form it takes, be it drugs or alcohol. Unworthiness, however, can stem from habits far less insidious than those. As we all know, we sometimes end up dealing with our feelings in rather peculiar ways that leave us with a sense of self-disgust instead of a sense of pride—so we have to find a formula for dealing with these problems.

It is impossible to live a pleasant life without living wisely and well and justly. And it is impossible to live wisely and well and justly without living pleasantly. Epicurus, in the third century B.C., wrote, "A balanced life is the solution to the search for happiness." One hundred years earlier, Euripides expanded on those simple terms in 431 B.C., "of mortals there is no-one who is happy, if wealth flows in upon one, one may perhaps be luckier than one's neighbour but still not happy." Aristotle, the Greek philosopher and mathematician, believed that "happiness is an expression of the soul in considered actions." He also wrote in the fourth century, "Happiness depends upon ourselves."

Two thousand years later, the persuasion of Euripides was echoed in the writings of John Stuart Mill. In 1863, he wrote in his book, *Utilitarianism,* "unquestionably it is possible to do without happiness; it is done involuntarily by nineteen-twentieths of mankind." At the same time, Nietzsche, a European philosopher, advised, "We should consider every day lost on which we have not danced at least once. And we should call every truth false which was not accompanied by at least one laugh." Clearly, the balance of historic opinion suggests that happiness, if it is to be attained, is something that only the individual can obtain for him or herself. So how does the individual go about obtaining happiness?

It is the conscious decision to alter what you continually do that is really effective. We all have the internal voice that drones on advising us to do things we don't want to do. Sometimes there are several voices with conflicting views—so you have to untangle good voices from bad ones, encourage the right ones, discourage the wrong ones, slap the wrong ones down, learn to discriminate in favor of the good voices. It is similar to looking at pictures in an art gallery or museum: discover the good paintings, spend time with them, discover the bad paintings and move on quickly so you get in the habit of looking longer at the good ones—similarly with your voices. You are the only person who thinks inside yourself, so give yourself more credit. Congratulate yourself more often for the good things that you do. Spend no time thinking about your faults, simply try to avoid them when they occur.

Everything and everyone has a vibe or essence. If you want to be happy, surround yourself with objects and people with a good essence, reject or remove bad vibes. This will help your peace of mind enormously. Then move on to giving. If you have managed to tidy up your own internal argument, you won't be giving with guilt or sacrifice but rather peacefully, knowing why you want to give. It could be time, money, or food. It is no good just wanting to help other people, you have to be in a state where you can help other people. The point of the parable of the good Samaritan is that he was able to help a person, not that he just wished to help people in general. Help needs to be practical, whether it is support that is financial or moral.

Ethics are of paramount importance in corporate life in the twenty-first century. Success and failure of any one company are now interwoven with other companies and the corrupt behaviour of a few individuals affects millions of lives elsewhere— surely the best known examples of this currently are Enron, Arthur Andersen, and WorldCom. The old mechanistic systems have become slow and clumsy so the integrity of the individual is now paramount. People are shifting their own boundaries so fast they are even living and working in the same place with multiple identities—all the more reason to understand ethical codes.

The breakdown of trust is a societal malaise, and mistrust creates tremendous anxiety. To trust is to tell the truth, to be discreet, to hold secrets safe, and behave appropriately. Breaking a trust is very hard, if not impossible, to redeem; for some of us, it is simply non-negotiable. Those who act ethically are given trust and entrusted with information. "If one tells the truth sooner or later one is sure to be found out," said Oscar Wilde. Ethical behavior relies on moral codes and today we are breaking moral codes in pursuit of short-term goals. Mistrust puts the body's central nervous system under continuous strain. Whether it is the suspicion that the stranger coming toward you might mug you, or whether a friend of twenty years would be a reliable trustee for your financial affairs, one should be able to delve into one's intuition and experience to come up with sound judgments. Above all, trust is the firm belief in someone or something and accepting this without needing evidence.

In the business world, a company creates trust with its clients. Knowing a customer's preferences and delivering them can increase a customer's trust and loyalty despite the increasing available choices. Trust is crucial for repeat business and therefore the ethical route complements our long-term goals whether they are business or personal. The recent and massive breakdown in trust in the accounting and financial spheres is driving people from the markets and ultimately from business. To be trustworthy is to make the world a better place, however large or small that gesture may be.

There is not a gene or a chemical for happiness—it is a process. Neurotransmitters allow us to think and most thoughts are not in the present when we think them—vast amounts are in the past, and many are fantasies for the future. Much happiness is connected to memory. Remembering a happy event is like re-winding the film roll and adding sentimentality; our memories exaggerate a past event so it seems more vivid. The mind resists the moment because it allows time to control it. Past times and future times are easier to handle; they take you back and forth, but the middle ground is harder to achieve. Past pain resides in the emotional mind. To be free we have to be free of the need for our pain. Oddly some people feel safer with their problems, as if they might lose a part of themselves without them.

People try to pursue happiness especially when they are young; later in life they realize it is the simplest pleasures that become paramount. Happiness is accepting that some people can do things better than you can, and realizing that competing with others when they are more skilled simply won't work. It is also true that the more you practice the luckier you get, and skill comes from practice. Thomas Jefferson wrote, "It is neither wealth nor splendour, but tranquillity and occupation which give happiness." These words imply that using your skills to the fullest is happiness.

There is a lot of confusion between happiness and pleasure, which is continually explored by philosophers and psychologists. Yet to keep it simple, try to live life from the inside out, rather than seeking pleasures outside to quench the self-indulgent thirst. There is widespread loneliness in the world and learning to love profoundly and with compassion can melt such isolation.

Culturally, happiness is a difficult concept for many civilizations. Jews do not have a word for happiness. Life in their view is a continual conflict of suffering. Ethiopians don't have a word for depression. American and European writers for centuries have written about happiness but always there has been the feeling that too much happiness will bring about disaster, that the reward for happiness must be sadness. Of course life is not one level road. Anyone who has driven across a vast plain or prairie will know how boring that is. Life is a series of hills from which you can look out, and we call these hills happiness. Obviously where you have hills you will have valleys that enclose you; we call these valleys sadness. The trick is to really enjoy the views from the hills and create situations where the hills fill a larger part of your personal landscape than the valleys. As will happen more than once in a lifetime when you find yourself in a huge valley, just think about the views from the hills. The old saying about the man who grumbled incessantly because his shoes pinched and ceased his grumbling when he met a man with no feet, is forever true.

Regardless of our optimism and our positive attitude to life, we will always have a feeling of guilt about happiness; it is part of our cultural heritage. In the *Apocrypha ecclesiastics* [30:22], we find, "Gladness of heart is the life of man and the rejoicing of a man is the length of his days." St. Augustine, in the year 426, wrote, "Indeed man wishes to be happy even when he so lives to make happiness impossible." The doubt about the lasting quality of happiness was exactly expressed by Jules Barbey d'Aurevilly, a French writer, in 1847: "Happy men are grave, they carry their happiness cautiously, as they would a glass filled to the brim of which the slightest movement could cause to spill over or break." Henry Ward Beecher in 1887 wrote, "In this world, full often our joys are only the tender shadows which our sorrows cast." Byron took the same view as the others between 1819 and 1824 when he wrote in his work *Don Juan*, "All who joy would win must share it, happiness has born a twin." Cervantes in his work *Don Quixote* (1605-15) wrote, "It seldom happens that any felicity comes so pure as not to be tempered and alloyed by some measure of sorrow."

For us to work efficiently in the workplace we must first find happiness in our home. For the work that comes from sadness and distress is a manic work that, on occasion, can be brilliant, but is not the sustained work that is the stuff of industry. Industry needs a workforce who at all levels is thinking ahead. A relaxed mind can deal with emergency and monotony alike with calm and humor. Refugees from home in the workplace are neither of real use to their company or to their colleagues. Those who get great joy out of their work function more efficiently if they get great joy out of their homes as well. Those who are myopic about their work will try, as they grow older, to hold onto their jobs with a terrifying determination. Their assistants will be of poor quality. The fear of a person whose only love is his or her job will result in them refusing to have competition of quality anywhere near them, and as a result their companies will suffer.

In the end the best way to achieve happiness for yourself is by ensuring all those around you are happy. It is your attitude to other people that really matters; if you seek happiness, enjoy their success. If your hurt is backdated in a long-gone part of your life, it is harder to achieve contentment in the present. Buddhists talk of emptiness and bliss and of action without accumulation. They achieve this through meditation. They say if you have a pain or discomfort in your body the more you think about the pain then the more the discomfort, so if you can stop thinking about the pain it is a lesser sensation of pain, so you will not be led into negativity. Obviously if the pain is excruciating, this is another matter. To ease constant thinking, however, meditation is beneficial. The key to happiness is understanding the spiritual dimensions of the here and now. Meditators call this "Big Mind" which has no start or ending, but requires withdrawing your attention from the past and future. Your mind will try to escape, but with practice you can reach the state that Buddhists describe as emptiness and bliss. Equally the power of prayer is as enormous as it is universally known. Being busy jars with the happiness of serenity as this beautiful quote suggests, "Happiness is as a butterfly which when pursued is always beyond our grasp but which if you will sit down quietly may alight upon you."

Many people living today lead their lives in a constant disappointment as they expect more from the world and more from other people than they do from themselves. Albert Camus, the French existentialist and Nobel Prize-winning writer, wrote, "An intellectual is someone whose mind watches it." We often think only about our emotional responses whereas if we could simply focus on our particular goals, we might recover from the emotion of disappointments. Vague pictures of where we ought to be in our lives will not help to materialize these opportunities as a realistic specific expectation, but visualizing it can make it happen. The enigmatic power of the mind is rather like alchemy. Thought-forming can produce instant physical results. Happiness may well be a personality trait rather than just connected to a human being's reaction to happy events. Depressed people are less happy, but they are more realistic. Good moods can lead to overconfidence and therefore end up with mistakes. Bad moods tend to lead to more logical thought processes and perhaps more accuracy. In fact, often believing you can succeed may produce a luckier outcome. A simple aim of contentment is to try to be comfortable on a daily basis. Don't follow your moods but reason with them, watch how you react. Thought can create a mood and that mood might last a long time. Our memories will recall a mood, an atmosphere, and it can elicit memory as if rewinding a video. Our physical state may alter and re-enact the same sensation from years ago, a surge of satisfaction from our stomachs up towards our heads. This past memory will become associated with a present one.

Happiness is organizing your life so it means something. You can have anything but you cannot have everything, and coming to terms with that is part of the package of being alive. At the same time, if you continue to do what you've always done, you'll always get what you've always got, so do something else for a new result. Research suggests that if we find our tasks or each other boring, it is largely due to the quality of our concentration or conversation. In general, it is wise to open our minds to new opportunities. It is very easy to pursue the wrong goals in order to achieve contentment, and often we are vague about our true needs. We need to make deliberate happiness choices. As Lewis Carroll wrote, "If you don't know where you are going, any road will take you there."

Is destiny God's will or is it in our own hands to create the power to design our destiny? All major religions teach a form of truth, however different they may be. We know that the power of prayer is enormous, whatever or whichever one's belief. In our book, happiness is about taking responsibility for your own well-being, emotionally and spiritually as well as physically and mentally. William Jefferson said, "Life belongs to the living," and that means focusing on our actions. It means practicing kindness, finding our rhythm, striving for understanding, and using our imaginations. Our happiness is staked on our relationships with others and the vitality of our daily routines, and only by focusing on these will we empower ourselves with success at home, at work, and at life.

Train the mind to be optimistic and hope for happiness for anyone, including yourself. As the Dalai Lama says, "In worldly terms, in terms of our enjoying a happy day-to-day existence, the greater the level of calmness of our mind, the greater our peace of mind, the greater our ability to enjoy a happy and joyful life."

INDEX

ABOUT THE AUTHORS

SIR ROBERT ALISTAIR McALPINE's political career included service as Deputy Chairman of the Conservative and Unionist Party. He is a member of the House of Lords, and the author of *Once a Jolly Bagman* and *The New Machiavelli,* among many successful books. He lives in Monaco.

KATE DIXEY has a deliberately varied career: costume designer, acupuncturist, and consultant to international businesses on health and image presentation. She has taught at the Cranford University and Cranford School of Management. She lives in London.

ABOUT TEXERE

TEXERE seeks to become the most progressive and authoritative
voice in business publishing by cultivating and enhancing ideas
that will illuminate the global business landscape. Our name
defines the spirit of our vision: TEXERE is the ancient Latin verb
"to weave." In an increasingly global business community, we seek
to create an intersection where authors and readers can share the
best thinking and the latest ideas. We want to leverage the expertise
and insights of leading thinkers by weaving them with TEXERE's
capability to deliver them to the marketplace.

To learn more and become a part of our community, visit us at:
www.etexere.com and www.etexere.co.uk

ABOUT THE TYPE

This book was set in Adobe Garamond, a typeface
based on the original designs and matrices of the
French typecutter Claude Garamond (c.1490–1561).
It was drawn by Robert Slimbach and issued in digital form
by the Adobe Corporation in 1989. Garamond remains one of
the best-known exponents of Renaissance type design
at work in sixteenth-century Paris.

Printed and bound by Edwards Brothers, Inc.,
Ann Arbor, Michigan

Designed and composed by Kevin Hanek